LONGMAN L

The Tempest

William Shakespeare

Editor: Jackie Head

LONGMAN

New Longman Shakespeare Series

A Midsummer Night's Dream   0 582 42712 6
Henry V   0 582 42711 8
Macbeth   0 582 36580 5
Romeo and Juliet   0 582 36579 1
The Merchant of Venice   0 582 42713 4
Twelfth Night   0 582 36578 3

Contents

Introduction

Shakespeare's life and times

Shakespeare was born into a time of change. Important discoveries about the world were changing people's whole way of life, their thoughts and their beliefs. The fact that we know very little of Shakespeare's particular life story does not mean that we cannot step into his world.

What do we know about Shakespeare?

Imagine for a minute you are Shakespeare, born in 1564, the son of a businessman who is making his way in Stratford-upon-Avon. When you are thirteen, Francis Drake sets off on a dangerous sea voyage around the world, to prove that it is round, not flat, and to bring back riches. The trades people who pass in and out of your town bring with them stories of other countries, each with their own unique culture and language. You learn in school of ancient heroic myths taught through Latin and Greek, and often, to bring these stories alive, travelling theatres pass through the town acting, singing, performing, and bringing with them tales of London. But, at the age of fourteen your own world shifts a little under your feet; your father has got into serious debt, you find yourself having to grow up rather fast.

This is an unremarkable life so far – the death of your sisters is not an uncommon occurrence at this time, and even when you marry at eighteen, your bride already pregnant at the ceremony, you are not the first to live through life in this way. After your daughter, your wife gives birth to twins, a girl and a boy, one of whom dies when he is eleven. But before this, for some reason only you know, perhaps to do with some poaching you are involved in or because your marriage to a woman eight years older than you is having difficulties, you travel to London. There you eventually join the theatre, first as an actor and then as a writer. You write for the theatres in the inn yards, then for Queen Elizabeth in court, and when she dies, for King James I. As well as this you write for the large theatres which are being built in London: the Rose, the Globe, Blackfriars and the Swan. You die a rich man.

What did Shakespeare find in London?

When Shakespeare first travelled to London he found a city full of all that was best and worst in this new era of discovery. There was trade in expensive and fashionable items, a bubbling street life with street-theatre, pedlars of every sort, sellers of songs and poems. Industry was flourishing in textiles, mining, the manufacture of glass, iron and sugar. The place to be known was the court of Queen Elizabeth. She was unmarried and drew many admirers even in her old age, maintaining a dazzling social world with her at its centre. There were writers and poets, grasping what they could of the new world, building on the literature of other countries, charting the lingering death of medieval life and the chaotic birth of something new.

By contrast, Shakespeare also found poverty, death and disease. The plague, spread by rats, found an easy home in these narrow streets, often spilling over with dirt and sewage: it killed 15,000 people in London in 1592 alone. It was an overcrowded city: the increased demand for wool for trade brought about the enclosure of land in the countryside, and this, coupled with bad harvests, brought the peasants, thrown off their land and made poor, into London to seek wealth.

What was England like in Shakespeare's day?

England was a proud nation. Elizabeth would not tolerate rivals and destroyed her enemies. In 1587 she had Mary Queen of Scots executed for treason, and in 1588 her navy defeated a huge armada of ships from Spain. Both acts were prompted by religion. In maintaining the Protes-tant Church of England her father, King Henry VIII, had established, Elizabeth stood out against a strong Catholic Europe. Within the Protestant religion too, there were divisions, producing extreme groups such as the Puritans who believed that much of the Elizabethan social scene was sinful, the theatres being one of their clearest targets for disapproval. Her power was threatened for other reasons too. In 1594 her doctor was executed for attempting to poison her, and in 1601 one of her favourites, the Earl of Essex, led an unsuccessful revolt against her.

When Elizabeth died in 1603 and James I succeeded her, he brought a change. He was a Scottish king, and traditionally Scotland and England had had an uneasy relationship. He was interested in witchcraft and he supported the arts, but not in the same way as Elizabeth had. He too met with treason, in the shape of Guy Fawkes and his followers, who in 1605 attempted to blow up the Houses of Parliament. If Shakespeare needed examples of life at its extremes, he had them all around him, and his closeness to the court meant he understood them more than most.

What other changes did Shakespeare see?

Towards the end of Shakespeare's life, in Italy, a man Shakespeare's age invented the telescope and looked at the stars. His radical discoveries caused him to be thrown out of the Catholic Church. For fifteen centuries people had believed in a picture of the universe as held in crystal spheres with order and beauty, and everything centring around the earth. In this belief the sun, moon and stars were the heavens; they ruled human fate, they were distant and magical. Galileo proved this was not so. So, the world was no longer flat and the earth was not the centre of the universe. It must have felt as if nothing was to be trusted anymore.

What do Shakespeare's plays show us about Elizabethan life?

Even without history books much of Shakespeare's life can be seen in his plays. They are written by one who knows of the tragedy of sudden death, and illness, and of the splendour of the life of the court in contrast to urban and rural poverty. He knows the ancient myths of the Greeks and Romans, the history of change in his own country, and, perhaps from reading the translations carried by merchants to London, he knows the literature of Spain and Italy.

His plays also contain all the hustle and bustle of normal life at the time. We see the court fool, the aristocracy, royalty, merchants and the servant classes. We hear of bear-baiting, fortune-telling, entertaining, drinking, dancing and singing. As new changes happen they are brought into the plays, in the form of maps, clocks, or the latest fashions. Shakespeare wrote to perform, and his plays were performed to bring financial reward. He studied his audience closely and produced what they wanted. Sometimes, as with the focus on witchcraft in **Macbeth** written for King James I, this was the celebration of something which fascinated them; sometimes, as with the character of Shylock in **The Merchant of Venice**, it was the mockery of something they despised.

What do Shakespeare's plays tell us about life now?

You can read Shakespeare's plays to find out about Elizabethan life, but in them you will also see reflected back at you the unchanging aspects of humanity. It is as if in all that changed around him, Shakespeare looked for the things that would *not* change – like love, power, honour, friendship and loyalty – and put them to the test. In each he found strength and weakness.

We see *love*:

- which is one-sided,
- between young lovers,
- in old age,
- between members of one family,
- lost and found again.

We see *power*:

- used and abused,
- in those who seek it,
- in those who protect it with loyalty,
- in the just and merciful rule of wise leaders,
- in the hands of unscrupulous tyrants.

We see *honour*:

- in noble men and women,
- lost through foolishness,
- stolen away through trickery and disloyalty.

We see *friendship*:

- between men and men, women and women, men and women,
- between masters and servants,
- put to the test of jealousy, grief and misunderstanding.

These are just some examples of how Shakespeare explored in his plays what it was to be human. He lived for fifty-two years and wrote thirty-seven plays, as well as a great number of poems. Just in terms of output this is a remarkable achievement. What is even more remarkable is the way in which he provides a window for his audiences into all that is truly human, and it is this quality that often touches us today.

What are Comedies, Tragedies and Histories?

When Shakespeare died, his players brought together the works he had written, and had them published. Before this some of the plays had only really existed as actors' scripts written for their parts alone. Many plays in Shakespeare's day and before were not written down at all, but spoken, and kept in people's memories from generation to generation. So, making accurate copies of Shakespeare's plays was not easy and there is still much dispute over how close to the original scripts our current editions are. Ever since they were first published people have tried to make sense of them.

Sometimes they are described under three headings: Comedy, Tragedy and History. The dates on the chart that follows refer to the dates of the first recorded performances or, if this is not known, the date of first publication. They may have been performed earlier but history has left us no record; dating the plays exactly is therefore difficult.

COMEDY	HISTORY	TRAGEDY
	King John (1590)	
	Henry VI, Part I (1592)	
Comedy of Errors (1594) *The Taming of the Shrew* (1594) *Two Gentlemen of Verona* (1594)		*Titus Andronicus* (1594)
The Merry Wives of Windsor (1597)	*Richard II* (1597) *Richard III* (1597)	*Romeo and Juliet* (1597)
The Merchant of Venice (1598) *Love's Labour's Lost* (1598)	*Henry IV, Part II* (1598)	
As You Like it (1600) *A Midsummer Night's Dream* (1600) *Much Ado About Nothing* (1600) *Twelfth Night* (1600)	*Henry V* (1600) *Henry VI, Part II* (1600) *Henry VI, Part III* (1600)	
Troilus and Cressida (1601)		
		Hamlet (1602)
Measure for Measure (1604) *All's Well That Ends Well* (1604)	*Henry IV, Part I* (1604)	*Othello* (1604)

COMEDY	HISTORY	TRAGEDY
		Julius Caesar (1605)
		Macbeth (1606)
		King Lear (1606)
		Antony and Cleopatra (1608)
		Timon of Athens (1608)
		Coriolanus (1608)
Pericles (1609)		
Cymbeline (1611)		
The Winter's Tale (1611)		
The Tempest (1611/12)	*Henry VIII* (1612)	

Comedy = a play which maintains a thread of joy throughout and ends happily for most of its characters.

Tragedy = a play in which characters must struggle with circumstances and in which most meet death and despair.

History = a play focusing on a real event or series of events which actually happened in the past.

These three headings can be misleading. Many of the comedies have great sadness in them, and there is humour in most of the tragedies, some of which at least point to happier events in the future. Some of the tragedies, like **Hamlet** and **Julius Caesar**, make history their starting point.

We do not know exactly when each play was written but from what we know of when they were performed we can see that Shakespeare began by writing poetry, then histories and comedies. He wrote most of his tragedies in the last ten years of his life, and in his final writings wrote stories full of near-tragic problems which, by the end of the plays he resolved. Sometimes these final plays (**Pericles**, **Cymbeline, The Winter's Tale** and **The Tempest**) are called Comedies, sometimes they are called Romances or simply The Late Plays.

Where were Shakespeare's plays performed?

Plays in Shakespeare's day were performed in several places, not just in specially designed theatres.

Inn Yard Theatres: Players performed in the open courtyard of Eliza-bethan inns. These were places where people could drink, eat and stay the night. They were popular places to make a break in a journey and to change or rest horses. Some inns built a permanent platform in the yard, and the audience could stand in the yard itself, or under shelter in the galleries which overlooked the yard. The audiences were lively and used to the active entertainment of bear-baiting, cock-fighting, wrestling and juggling. Plays performed here needed to be action-packed and appealing to a wide audience. In 1574 new regulations were made to control performances in response to the number of fights which regularly broke out in the audience.

Private House Theatres: The rich lords of Elizabethan times would pay travelling theatre companies to play in the large rooms of their own private houses for the benefit of their friends. There was no stage and the audience were all seated. Torches and candles were used to create artificial lighting. Costumes played an important part in creating atmos-phere but there were no sets.

Public Hall Theatres: Some town councils would allow performances of plays in their grand halls and council buildings. As well as this, ceremonial halls such as the Queen's courts in Whitehall were frequently used in this way, as were halls at Hampton Court, Richmond and Greenwich Palace. For these performances, designed for a larger audience than those given in private houses, scaffolding would be arranged for tiered seating which would surround a central acting area. Audiences were limited to those with a high social standing.

Public Theatres: Unlike Public Hall theatres, these theatres were built for the purpose of presenting plays. At the end of the sixteenth century there were about 200,000 people living in London, and eleven public theatres showing performances. Of these, about half a dozen were so large that they seated about 2,000 people. The audiences, who were drawn from all sections of society, paid to see performances which began at 2 p.m. The audience sat in covered galleries around a circular acting area which was open air. Whilst the theatres stood within the City of London they were subject to its laws. They could not perform during times of worship, and they were closed during outbreaks of the plague. Theatres were often the scenes of fighting and because of the trouble this caused, in 1596 performances of plays were forbidden within the city boundaries. Thus, people started building theatres outside the city on the south side of the River Thames.

What were the performances like?

To some extent this depended on the play being performed and the audience watching. A play performed before the court of the queen or king would need to be one that did not offend the ruler. Plays performed in the inn yard or the public theatres needed to have a wide appeal and several distractions such as dancing and music to keep the audience's attention.

Wherever they performed, the players had to create the illusion that the whole world could be seen inside their play. They had no sets, except in some cases tapestries which were hung up to show changes in scenery, but they did have bright costumes in which to perform. Scenes of battle or shipwreck were suggested by words rather than special effects, though we do know that they used burning torches, as it was due to a fire caused by one of these that the first Globe Theatre burnt down during a performance in 1613.

Actors joined together in companies, who would perform several different plays, and be sponsored by the nobility. Shakespeare became a key member of the Lord Chamberlain's company which Queen Elizabeth sponsored, and which went on to be called The King's Men when James I became king.

There were no women on the Elizabethan stage. Most female characters would be played by boys whose voices had not yet broken, or if it was an old character, by men in the company. Actors carried a reputation for being immoral and ungodly people, and were therefore thought unsuitable company for women. The men of Shakespeare's company became famous for playing particular types of characters such as the fool, the lover or the villain. Shakespeare probably created many of his parts with particular actors in mind.

Where can I find out more about Shakespeare?

Shakespeare is perhaps the world's most famous playwright and there is no shortage of books written about him. In your library or bookshop you will find books which look at:

- Shakespeare's life;

- the history of England under the reign of Queen Elizabeth I and James I;

- European history, art and literature of the sixteenth and seventeenth century;

- discoveries made throughout the world during Elizabethan times;

- characters, themes and ideas in Shakespeare's writing.

In Stratford-upon-Avon you can visit his birthplace, and much of the town consists of buildings which would have stood in Shakespeare's day. In addition to this there are many museums and exhibitions which tell more about Shakespeare's life and work.

Some theatrical companies today, such as the Royal Shakespeare Company, devote themselves to performing Shakespeare's plays in

London, Stratford, and on tour around the country. They are always seeking new ways to bring the plays to life. However, perhaps the best way to find out more about Shakespeare is to study his plays by reading and acting them yourself. Shakespeare wrote about what he knew, and the key to discovering how his mind and emotions worked is to look at what he wrote.

Shakespeare's language

Speaking Shakespeare

The Tempest was written as a play, so the lines should be heard and not just seen. Speaking the lines can sound strange to start with, so the best thing to do is practise.

Below are some extracts from the play to start you off.
Remember:

- Pause at commas, colons and semi-colons.
- Take a breath at the end of sentences (that is at full stops not at the end of lines).
- Try to follow the meaning of the words and place the emphasis on appropriate words in order to get the meaning across.
- Try to read at normal speaking pace (not quicker or slower).
- Don't worry if you make mistakes, everyone does!

Angry one-liners

Here are some one line insults from the play. Can you get the rude phrases to sound just right?

SEBASTIAN

  A pox o' your throat, you bawling, blasphemous, incharitable dog!

(Act 1, scene 1, lines 40–1)

PROSPERO

  Thou liest, malignant thing!

(Act 1, scene 2, line 257)

CALIBAN

> You taught me language; and my profit on 't
> Is, I know how to curse. The red plague rid you
> For learning me your language!

(Act I, scene 2, lines 365–7)

A musical speech

Stephano and Trinculo are scared by the music created by the spirit Ariel. Caliban, who has lived on the island all his life, reassures them that there is nothing to be scared of:

CALIBAN

> Be not afeard; the isle is full of noises,
> Sounds and sweet airs, that give delight, and hurt not.
> Sometimes a thousand twangling instruments
> Will hum about mine ears; and sometime voices,
> That, if I then had waked after a long sleep,
> Will make me sleep again. And then, in dreaming,
> The clouds methought would open, and show riches
> Ready to drop upon me; that, when I waked,
> I cried to dream again.

(Act 3, scene 2, lines 137–45)

A funny word-play

Gonzalo and Adrian describe the island as a paradise. Antonio and Sebastian, who can see little joy in being shipwrecked there, mock his speech.

ADRIAN

> The air breathes upon us here most sweetly.

SEBASTIAN

> As if it had lungs, and rotten ones.

ANTONIO

> Or as 't were perfumed by a fen.

GONZALO
  Here is everything advantageous to life.

ANTONIO
  True; save means to live.

SEBASTIAN
  Of that there 's none, or little.

GONZALO
  How lush and lusty the grass looks! How green!

ANTONIO
  The ground, indeed, is tawny.

SEBASTIAN
  With an eye of green in 't.

ANTONIO
  He misses not much.

SEBASTIAN
  No; he doth but mistake the truth totally.

(Act 2, scene 1, lines 44–54)

A romantic speech

Miranda is in love with Ferdinand and wants to know if he loves her.

MIRANDA
  Do you love me?

FERDINAND
  O heaven, O earth, bear witness to this sound
  And crown what I profess with kind event,
  If I speak true! if hollowly, invert
  What best is boded me to mischief! I,
  Beyond all limit of what else i' the world,
  Do love, prize, honour you.

(Act 3, scene 1, lines 67–73)

A speech of despair

Alonso, having looked wearily for his son, finally gives up hope of his being alive.

GONZALO

             By your patience,

I needs must rest me.

ALONSO

             Old lord, I cannot blame thee,

Whom am myself attached with weariness

To the dulling of my spirits. Sit down, and rest.

Even here I will put off my hope, and keep it

No longer for my flatterer. He is drowned

Whom thus we stray to find; and the sea mocks

Our frustrate search on land. Well, let him go.

                         (Act 3, scene 3, lines 3–10)

Prose and blank verse

Every play by Shakespeare is written partly in *prose* (ordinary written language) and partly in *verse*, which may or may not rhyme. If it does not rhyme, it is called *blank verse*. Most of the verse in the play has ten beats to each line. Blank verse is generally spoken by the nobility in Shakespeare's plays and prose by the servant classes.

However in the late plays (of which **The Tempest** is one), Shakespeare seems to break his own rules about this. Trinculo (the king's jester), Stephano (the king's butler), and the boatswain all speak in prose. Prospero, the rightful Duke of Milan speaks in blank verse as do the other characters of noble birth. However Ariel and Caliban, Prospero's servants who have been taught language by him, often speak in blank verse.

One complete exception to this is during the first scene of the play when the characters, who are on board a ship that is breaking up in a storm, speak a mixture of verse and prose. This helps to get across the sense that the storm has thrown everything into complete chaos.

In **The Tempest** Ferdinand is separated from his father, the king, and believes him to be dead. In Act 1, scene 2, lines 390–8 he hears music created by Ariel, and wonders what effect it has on him. Try reading the lines out loud a few times and get a partner to count the number of beats in each line:

Where should this music be? I' th' air or th' earth?	1
It sounds no more; and, sure, it waits upon	2
Some god o' th' island. Sitting on a bank,	3
Weeping again the King my father's wrack,	4
This music crept by me upon the waters,	5
Allaying both their fury and my passion	6
With its sweet air. Thence I have follow'd it,	7
Or it hath drawn me rather. But 't is gone.	8
No, it begins again.	9

Lines 3 to 8 are in fact one sentence (with only one full stop) but each line begins with a capital letter. We can see from line 3 that sentences do not have to finish at the end of lines but might end halfway through a line. So, when you're reading the words you should read them in sentences, following full stops and not the capital letters.

Sometimes Shakespeare used shortened words to make the beats fit, as in line 1, where 'I' th' air' is used instead of 'in the air', and in line 3, where 'o' th' island' is used instead of 'of the island'. In Shakespeare's plays words ending in 'ed' such as 'purged' and 'blessed', have the 'ed' sounded out as a separate syllable. If Shakespeare didn't want this extra syllable to sound then he would shorten the word 'purg'd' and 'bless'd', as he has done with 'follow'd' in line 7.

Blank verse is very flexible. It sounds almost like normal speech but it gives the words a more musical and refined quality. For this reason it is often the nobility in Shakespeare's plays who speak in blank verse, and the servant classes who speak in prose.

In **The Tempest** Caliban has been taught language by Prospero. He uses it but at the same time hates the fact that it is Prospero's language. His speech is full of curses and its form is partly blank verse or a sort of semi-blank verse using not quite the right number of syllables.

CALIBAN

    All the infections that the sun sucks up
    From bogs, fens, flats, on Prosper fall, and make him
    By inch-meal a disease! His spirits hear me,
    And yet I needs must curse. But they'll nor pinch,
    Fright me with urchin-shows, pitch me i' the mire,
    Nor lead me, like a firebrand, in the dark
    Out of my way, unless he bid 'em. But
    For every trifle are they set upon me;
    Sometimes like apes, that mow and chatter at me,
    And after bite me; then like hedgehogs, which
    Lie tumbling in my barefoot way, and mount
    Their pricks at my footfall; sometime am I
    All wound with adders, who with cloven tongues
    Do hiss me into madness.

                      (Act 2, scene 2, lines 1–14)

As you read the play, take note of:

- which characters normally speak in verse;
- which characters normally speak in prose;
- which circumstances cause characters to change their normal speech form.

Images

You will have seen from the extracts you have read already, that Shakespeare makes his words as full of meaning as possible. He often gets a character to tell a story that is so rich in ideas it is more like a painting. These pictures are formed by the use of *figurative language* such as similes and metaphors.

In Act 4, scene 1, Ariel tells Prospero how Trinculo, Stephano and Caliban have followed his voice through prickly bushes, as a calf follows unquestioningly the lowing of its mother. For this image he uses a simile: 'calf-like'. You can spot *similes* because they usually use the words 'like' or 'as'.

> So I charmed their ears,
> That, calf-like, they my lowing followed, through
> Toothed briers, sharp furzes, pricking goss, and thorns,
> Which entered their frail shins.

(lines 178–81)

A *metaphor* is also a compressed comparison of two objects (like the calf and the men above) but it does not use the words 'like' or 'as'. It describes something as being another.

In Act 1, scene 2 of the play, Prospero describes the villainy of his brother Antonio who steals the dukedom and realises his ambitions by destroying the rightful duke, just as an ivy will grow over the trunk of a tree and in doing so will hide the trunk completely, eventually destroying it.

> new created
> The creatures that were mine, I say, or changed them,
> Or else new formed them; having both the key
> Of officer and office, set all hearts i' the state
> To what tune pleased his ear; that now he was
> The ivy which had hid my princely trunk,
> And sucked my verdure out on 't.

(lines 81–7)

One noticeable feature of **The Tempest** is the way in which Shakespeare plays with word order, and compresses his speech so that it is full of images. Look out for Prospero's long sentences where the personal pronoun ('I') appears later than you would expect, such as in the following extract:

> The direful spectacle of the wrack, which touched
> The very virtue of compassion in thee,
> I have with such provision in mine Art
> So safely ordered that there is no soul –
> No, not so much perdition as an hair
> Betid to any creature in the vessel
> Which thou heard'st cry, which thou saw'st sink.

(Act 1, scene 2, line 26–32)

Look out for images which Shakespeare uses several times in the play. Do they build up a particular atmosphere or tell us something about a certain character?

Look, also, for the placing together of two nouns to produce interesting and dramatic images, such as 'sea-change', 'cloud-capped', 'hag-seed' and 'man-monster'.

Understanding the play

The practice extracts will have helped you to see how the language of the play is spoken. Speaking the words correctly and looking out for figurative language will also help you to understand what the language means.

Here are some more ways to work out the meanings of words and phrases:

- The words themselves – are they similar to modern words? Can you guess their meaning from this? Check the glossary for words that are new to you.
- The context of the immediate lines – is there a general theme in the conversation/speech, that might give you some clues?
- The context of the scene – where and when is this scene taking place? What is the main action? Can you picture the scene and pick up clues from the setting?
- The characters as you understand them – when you saw this character before was he or she funny, depressed, scared, serious? Can you guess at the sort of things this person might say and the sort of tone he or she is likely to adopt?

Don't worry if you don't understand every word. On your first reading, or hearing, what is important is getting the gist of what is being said. Shakespeare's language is very rich in its ideas and images. You do not have to understand it all at once: you can enjoy finding out more each time you revisit it.

The glossary: a word of warning

The glossary has been compiled to help you understand the language of the play. On occasions complex and beautiful poetry has been translated or paraphrased into mundane, straightforward prose. When this happens, some of the original meaning is bound to be lost. You are advised, therefore, to use the glossary as a help with your first reading, but once you feel you have the main gist of the meaning, you should try to rely on it less.

The Tempest

CHARACTERS
in the play

ALONSO, *King of Naples*
SEBASTIAN, *his brother*
PROSPERO, *the rightful Duke of Milan*
ANTONIO, *his brother, the usurping Duke of Milan*
FERDINAND, *Alonso's son*
GONZALO, *an honest old councillor*
ADRIAN
FRANCISCO } *lords*
CALIBAN, *a savage and deformed slave*
TRINCULO, *a jester*
STEPHANO, *a drunken butler*
MASTER OF A SHIP, BOATSWAIN, MARINERS, ATTENDANTS
MIRANDA, *Prospero's daughter*
ARIEL, *an airy spirit*
IRIS
CERES
JUNO } *spirits*
NYMPHS
REAPERS

———

The scenes are laid on a ship at sea and on an uninhabited island.

3

*Mark Rylance as Ariel and Michael Maloney as Ferdinand in the 1982 Royal Shakespeare Company production of the **The Tempest**.*

Act 1: summary

During a storm at sea, Alonso the king of Naples and his men are struggling for their lives as their ship threatens to break up. Living on the island where the ship founders, are Prospero and his daughter Miranda. Prospero has learned the art of magic and caused the storm to bring on to the island all those who have previously wronged him. Miranda suspects he is responsible for it and wants to know why.

Prospero tells Miranda the story of his life. Twelve years ago he was the Duke of Milan, but enjoying his solitude and learning, he handed over many of the duties of the dukedom to his brother Antonio. Eventually Antonio turned against Prospero, and with the help of Alonso, the King of Naples, banished Prospero. Antonio made himself the new Duke of Milan and forced Prospero to set sail in a broken-down boat, with his three-year-old daughter Miranda. One of Prospero's servants, Gonzalo, smuggled provisions and some of Prospero's books on to the boat and these ensured their survival until they landed on the island.

Prospero calls his spirit-servant Ariel who describes the effect the storm has had. The passengers and crew are scattered in groups around the island, each believing they are the only survivors. Ariel reminds Prospero that the latter has promised to free him, but Prospero recalls how the island was once ruled by a witch, Sycorax, who had a child (Caliban) by a devil and then died, leaving Ariel a captive in a tree. Without Prospero, Ariel would still be imprisoned. Caliban hates Prospero, believing that the latter has stolen the island from him. However Prospero has taught Caliban to speak and always showed him human kindness until Caliban tried to rape Miranda.

Ariel sings to Ferdinand telling him that his father, the king, is dead, and with the music he leads Ferdinand to Miranda. The two fall in love at first sight. Prospero pretends that Ferdinand is a spy and orders him to carry wood for him. Prospero then congratulates himself and Ariel on the magic they have used.

1 **Boatswain**   sailor in charge of the crew.

2 **What cheer?**   how are you?

3 **mariners**   sailors.

   Fall to it, yarely   do it quickly.

4 **we run**   we will run.

   Bestir, bestir   move yourself, get going.

5 **Heigh**   come on.

   my hearts   a term of endearment, such as 'my good fellows'.

6 **Yare**   be alert.

   Tend   listen to.

10 **Play**   direct.

11 **below**   on the lower decks of the ship.

Act One

Scene one

On a ship. A storm with thunder and lightning.

Enter a SHIP-MASTER *and a* BOATSWAIN.

MASTER
  Boatswain!

BOATSWAIN
  Here, Master. What cheer?

MASTER
  Good. Speak to the mariners. Fall to it, yarely, or
  we run ourselves aground. Bestir, bestir.

Exit

Enter MARINERS.

BOATSWAIN
  Heigh, my hearts! Cheerly, cheerly, my hearts!   5
  Yare, yare! Take in the topsail. Tend to the Master's
  whistle. (*To the storm*) Blow till thou burst thy
  wind, if room enough!

Exeunt MARINERS

Enter ALONSO, SEBASTIAN, ANTONIO, FERDINAND, GONZALO, *and
others.*

ALONSO
  Good boatswain, have care. Where 's the Master?
  Play the men.   10

BOATSWAIN
  I pray now, keep below.

12 **bosun**   sailor in charge of the crew.

13 **mar our labour**   interfere with our work.

14 **You do assist the storm**   by coming on to the upper decks the noblemen are getting in the way of the sailors and thus increase the risks already brought about by the storm.

15 **Nay**   no.

   good   a courteous form of address; 'good man'.

16 **When**   I will (be patient) when.

   Hence!   go from here.

16–17 **What cares these . . . of King?**   the angry sea has no respect for the king, it treats all men the same.

19 **whom thou hast aboard**   who is on board the ship.

21 **councillor**   member of the king's council, a respected advisor.

22 **work the peace of the present**   bring us peace now.

23 **hand a rope more**   handle another rope.

25–6 **for the mischance . . . so hap**   for the possibility of the worst occurring.

28–9 **Methinks . . . upon him**   I think he is not likely to die of drowning. The position of a mole ('mark') on the body was supposed to indicate the way in which a person would die.

29–30 **His . . . gallows**   he has the face of a man who'll hang.

30–3 **Stand fast . . . miserable**   if he is fated to hang let this come to pass (i.e. don't let him drown or we will too). We'll hang on to this hope as if it is an anchor to save us. If he is not destined to be hanged, we'll drown.

ANTONIO

Where is the Master, bosun?

BOATSWAIN

Do you not hear him? You mar our labour. Keep your cabins. You do assist the storm.

GONZALO

Nay, good, be patient.   15

BOATSWAIN

When the sea is. Hence! What cares these roarers for the name of King? To cabin! Silence! Trouble us not.

GONZALO

Good, yet remember whom thou hast aboard.

BOATSWAIN

None that I more love than myself. You are a   20
councillor. If you can command these elements to silence and work the peace of the present, we will not hand a rope more. Use your authority. If you cannot, give thanks you have lived so long, and make yourself ready in your cabin for the   25
mischance of the hour, if it so hap. Cheerly, good hearts! Out of our way, I say.

Exit

GONZALO

I have great comfort from this fellow. Methinks he hath no drowning mark upon him. His complexion is perfect gallows. Stand fast, good   30
Fate, to his hanging. Make the rope of his destiny our cable, for our own doth little advantage. If he be not born to be hanged, our case is miserable.

Exeunt

34–5 **Bring her . . . main-course**   sail close to the wind.

35–6 **A plague upon**   damn them for. The plague was a highly infectious disease which killed many people in Shakespeare's day.

36–7 **They are . . . office**   the cries of the passengers are louder than the storm and the men cannot hear their orders.

38 **give o'er**   give in.

39 **Have you a mind to sink?**   do you intend to drown?

40 **A pox o' your throat**   may you get venereal disease.

    blasphemous   swearing against God.

42 **Work you**   you do the work.

43 **Hang**   may you be hanged.

    cur   dog.

    whoreson   child of a prostitute.

    insolent   rude.

45 **thou art**   you are.

46 **I'll warrant . . . though**   I'll guarantee he won't drown, even if.

48 **unstanched**   unable to hold water, i.e. incontinent.

49 **Lay her a-hold**   sail the ship close to the wind.

    two courses   i.e. foresail and mainsail.

Enter BOATSWAIN.

BOATSWAIN

Down with the topmast! Yare! Lower, lower! Bring
her to try with main-course. *(A cry within)* A plague   35
upon this howling! They are louder than the
weather or our office.

Enter SEBASTIAN, ANTONIO, *and* GONZALO.

Yet again! What do you here? Shall we give o'er,
and drown? Have you a mind to sink?

SEBASTIAN

A pox o' your throat, you bawling, blasphemous,   40
incharitable dog!

BOATSWAIN

Work you, then.

ANTONIO

Hang, cur! Hang, you whoreson, insolent noise-
maker. We are less afraid to be drowned than
thou art.   45

GONZALO

I 'll warrant him for drowning, though the ship
were no stronger than a nutshell, and as leaky
as an unstanched wench.

BOATSWAIN

Lay her a-hold, a-hold! Set her two courses; off to
sea again; lay her off.   50

Enter MARINERS *wet.*

MARINERS

All lost! To prayers, to prayers! All lost!

52 **must our mouths be cold?**   are we going to die? This may refer to sailors drinking if the work was hard and risky, thus warming their mouths with alcohol.

54 **case is as**   position is the same as.

56 **wide-chapped**   wide-mouthed; presumably the sailor was drinking.

58 **The washing of ten tides**   captured pirates would be hanged on the sea shore and left there for three tides. Antonio wishes even greater punishment for the boatswain.

58–60 **He'll be hanged . . . glut him**   even though it would seem he was to drown in this storm, he will hang (as a villain) and, like the pirate, be left to swallow sea water until he bursts.

61 **We split**   the boat is splitting in the storm.

65 **take leave**   say farewell and leave.

66 **furlongs**   a furlong is ten square acres.

68 **The wills above**   the gods' desires.

69 **fain**   gladly.

BOATSWAIN

What, must our mouths be cold?

GONZALO

The King and Prince at prayers. Let 's assist them,
For our case is as theirs.

SEBASTIAN

I'm out of patience.

ANTONIO

We are merely cheated of our lives by drunkards.   55
This wide-chapped rascal - (*To the* BOATSWAIN) Would
thou mightst lie drowning,
The washing of ten tides!

GONZALO

He 'll be hanged yet,
Though every drop of water swear against it,
And gape at wid'st to glut him.   60

(*A confused noise within*) 'Mercy on us!' – 'We split,
we split!' – 'Farewell, my wife and children!' –
'Farewell, brother!' – 'We split, we split, we split!'

ANTONIO

Let's all sink with the King.

SEBASTIAN

Let's take leave of him.   65

Exeunt ANTONIO *and* SEBASTIAN

GONZALO

Now would I give a thousand furlongs of sea for an
acre of barren ground, long heath, broom, furze,
anything. The wills above be done! But I would
fain die a dry death.

Exeunt

13

1   **Art**   magic.

2   **allay**   weaken, still.

3   **stinking pitch**   a foul black tarry substance.

4   **But that**   if it weren't for the fact that.

     mounting . . . cheek   raised up to the sky by the storm.

7   **creature**   person.

8–9   **knock . . . heart**   tore at my heart strings; affected me greatly.

9   **perished**   died.

11–12   **or ere It**   or else the earth.

13   **fraughting . . . her**   the people who were on board, literally the cargo or freight.

     Be collected   calm yourself.

14   **piteous**   compassionate.

16   **in care of thee**   for your good.

17–18   **who . . . thou art**   Miranda does not know herself, or many things about herself.

19   **Of whence I am**   where I come from.

     more better   a nobler man.

20   **full poor**   meagre.

21   **thy no greater father**   no more than your father.

Scene two - The exposition scene.

Outside Prospero's cell on the island.

Enter PROSPERO *and* MIRANDA.

MIRANDA

    If by your Art, my dearest father, you have
    Put the wild waters in this roar, allay them.
    The sky, it seems, would pour down stinking pitch,
    But that the sea, mounting to the welkin's cheek,
    Dashes the fire out. Oh, I have suffered   5
    With those that I saw suffer! A brave vessel,
    Who had, no doubt, some noble creature in her,
    Dashed all to pieces. Oh, the cry did knock
    Against my very heart! Poor souls, they perished.
    Had I been any god of power, I would   10
    Have sunk the sea within the earth, or ere
    It should the good ship so have swallowed, and
    The fraughting souls within her.

PROSPERO

                          Be collected.
    No more amazement. Tell your piteous heart
    There 's no harm done.

MIRANDA

                Oh, woe the day!

PROSPERO

                       No harm.   15
    I have done nothing but in care of thee –
    Of thee, my dear one; thee, my daughter – who
    Art ignorant of what thou art; nought knowing
    Of whence I am, nor that I am more better
    Than Prospero, master of a full poor cell,   20
    And thy no greater father.

21–2 **More to know . . . thoughts**   it never entered my head that there was any more to know.

  22 **'T**   it.

  24 **inform thee farther**   give you more information.

  25 **Art**   magic.

  26 **direful spectacle**   terrible picture.

       wrack   shipwreck.

26–7 **touched . . . in thee**   awoke all your noblest feelings of compassion.

  28 **with such . . . Art**   through my magic.

29–31 **no soul . . . vessel**   no one – no, not a single person on that ship has lost so much as one hair from his head.

  33 **farther**   more.

  35 **bootless inquisition**   pointless questioning.

  36 **Stay**   wait.

  37 **ope thine ear**   listen.

40–1 **thou wast not Out**   you were not quite.

MIRANDA
                              More to know
Did never meddle with my thoughts.

PROSPERO
                                        'T is time
I should inform thee farther. Lend thy hand,
And pluck my magic garment from me. – So. *(He
    lays his mantle down.)*
Lie there, my Art. Wipe thou thine eyes. Have
    comfort.   25
The direful spectacle of the wrack, which touched
The very virtue of compassion in thee,
I have with such provision in mine Art
So safely ordered that there is no soul –
No, not so much perdition as an hair   30
Betid to any creature in the vessel
Which thou heard'st cry, which thou saw'st sink.
    Sit down;
For thou must now know farther.

MIRANDA
                              You have often
Begun to tell me what I am, but stopped,
And left me to a bootless inquisition,   35
Concluding 'Stay; not yet.'

PROSPERO
                        The hour 's now come.
The very minute bids thee ope thine ear.
Obey, and be attentive. Canst thou remember
A time before we came unto this cell?
I do not think thou canst, for then thou wast not   40
Out three years old.

42 **By what?** what is it that helps you to remember?

43–4 **Of any thing . . . remembrance** tell me any picture you have that stays in your memory.

45 **rather like** more like.

45–6 **than an . . . warrants** than proof that I have remembered.

47 **tended** looked after.

49 **What seest thou** what else do you see?

50 **backward** past.

abysm bottomless depths, abyss.

51 **aught ere** anything before.

52 **How thou . . . mayst** you might remember how you came here.

56 **piece of virtue** perfect example of goodness.

57 **thou wast** you were.

59 **no worse issued** no less nobly born.

MIRANDA

Certainly, sir, I can!

PROSPERO

By what? By any other house or person?
Of any thing the image tell me that
Hath kept with thy remembrance.

MIRANDA

'T is far off,
And rather like a dream than an assurance   45
That my remembrance warrants. Had I not
Four or five women once that tended me?

PROSPERO

Thou hadst, and more, Miranda. But how is it
That this lives in thy mind? What seest thou else
In the dark backward and abysm of time?   50
If thou rememb'rest aught ere thou cam'st here,
How thou cam'st here thou mayst.

MIRANDA

But that I do not.

PROSPERO

Twelve year since, Miranda, twelve year since,
Thy father was the Duke of Milan, and
A prince of power.

MIRANDA

Sir, are not you my father?   55

PROSPERO

Thy mother was a piece of virtue, and
She said thou wast my daughter, and thy father
Was Duke of Milan; and his only heir
And princess, no worse issued.

60 **What foul play had we**   what evil deeds were carried out against us.
   thence   there.

61 **Or blessèd . . . did**   or where we blessed to have left there?

62 **thou say'st**   you say.

63 **holp hither**   helped here, brought here.

64 **o' the teen**   of the grief.
   turned you to   brought to you.

65 **from my remembrance**   forgotten by me.
   farther   tell me more.

67 **mark me**   listen to me.

68 **perfidious**   unfaithful.
   next thyself   next to you.

69–70 **put . . . of my state**   gave the management of my dukedom.

71 **signories**   one of the states of northern Italy.

72 **prime**   first, highest in status.
   reputed   highly thought of.

73 **for the liberal arts**   arts considered to be worthy of a noble man.

75 **cast upon**   gave over to.

76 **to my state grew stranger**   became less involved with the usual duties of a
   duke.

76–7 **transported And rapt**   passionately involved.

77 **false**   corrupt, deceitful.

MIRANDA

                    Oh, the heavens!
What foul play had we, that we came from
    thence?   60
Or blesséd was 't we did?

PROSPERO

                 Both, both, my girl:
By foul play, as thou say'st, were we heaved thence,
But blessedly holp hither.

MIRANDA

                  Oh, my heart bleeds
To think o' the teen that I have turned you to,
Which is from my remembrance! Please you,
    farther.   65

PROSPERO

My brother, and thy uncle, called Antonio –
I pray thee, mark me, that a brother should
Be so perfidious! – he whom next thyself
Of all the world I loved, and to him put
The manage of my state; as at that time   70
Through all the signories it was the first,
And Prospero the prime duke, being so reputed
In dignity, and for the liberal arts
Without a parallel. Those being all my study,
The government I cast upon my brother,   75
And to my state grew stranger, being transported
And rapt in secret studies. Thy false uncle –
Dost thou attend me?

MIRANDA

              Sir, most heedfully.

79 **Being once . . . suits**   having learnt how to agree to petitions.

80 **advance**   promote.

81 **To trash for over-topping**   to discipline for over-stepping their authority.

81–2 **new created . . . mine**   remolded my servants to serve him.

83–4 **both the key . . . office**   control over the position and the person.

84–5 **set all . . . ear**   persuaded everyone in the dukedom to play to his tune.

85–6 **he was . . . trunk**   as ivy grows on the tree trunk and eventually kills it, so Antonio lived off and endangered Prospero.

87 **verdure**   health, energy, power.

89 **thus neglecting worldly ends**   paying no attention to the concerns of the world.

90 **closeness**   seclusion, isolation.

91–3 **but by being . . . evil nature**   the fact that I was a recluse was beyond the understanding of my people and this allowed my disloyal brother to be evil.

94–6 **did beget . . . trust was**   made him produce an evil plan, as terrible as my trust was great.

97 **sans bound**   without restrictions.

lorded   made a lord.

98 **yielded**   produced.

99 **but what . . . exact**   but anything else my power might bring.

100 **Who having . . . telling of it**   who, by lying so frequently.

101 **sinner**   liar.

103–4 **Out o' . . . of royalty**   because he was my second in command and behaved as if he were royal.

105 **prerogative**   the rights (given to royalty).

PROSPERO

    Being once perfected how to grant suits,
    How to deny them, who t' advance, and who   80
    To trash for over-topping, new created
    The creatures that were mine, I say, or changed
      them,
    Or else new formed them; having both the key
    Of officer and office, set all hearts i' the state
    To what tune pleased his ear; that now he was   85
    The ivy which had hid my princely trunk,
    And sucked my verdure out on 't. Thou attend'st
      not?

MIRANDA

    O, good sir, I do.

PROSPERO

                I pray thee, mark me.
    I, thus neglecting worldly ends, all dedicated
    To closeness and the bettering of my mind   90
    With that which, but by being so retired,
    O'er-prized all popular rate, in my false brother
    Awaked an evil nature; and my trust,
    Like a good parent, did beget of him
    A falsehood in its contrary as great   95
    As my trust was; which had indeed no limit,
    A confidence sans bound. He being thus lorded,
    Not only with what my revenue yielded,
    But what my power might else exact, like one
    Who having into truth, by telling of it,   100
    Made such a sinner of his memory,
    To credit his own lie, he did believe
    He was indeed the duke. Out o' the substitution,
    And executing th' outward face of royalty,
    With all prerogative – hence his ambition

107 **To have no screen** in order that he should have no barrier.

108–9 **he needs . . . Milan** it was necessary for him to rule Milan, to be duke.

109–10 **my library . . . large enough** I had enough to concern me in my library.

110 **Of temporal royalties** the secular work of a ruler.

111–12 **confederates . . . sway, wi'** he was so concerned to rule and be allies with.

114 **Subject his . . . crown** place the dukedom in subservience to the kingdom.

114–15 **bend . . . yet unbowed** and bow down in service in a way the dukedom had never previously done.

117 **Mark his . . . event** take heed of the sort of man he is and what he has done.

121–2 **an enemy . . . inveterate** a long-standing and much-hated enemy.

122 **hearkens . . . suit** listens to my brother's plea.

123–4 **in lieu . . . homage** in return for such worship.

growing –   105
Dost thou hear?

MIRANDA

Your tale, sir, would cure deafness.

PROSPERO

To have no screen between this part he played
And him he played it for, he needs will be
Absolute Milan. Me, poor man, my library
Was dukedom large enough. Of temporal
   royalties   110
He thinks me now incapable; confederates,
So dry he was for sway, wi' the King of Naples
To give him annual tribute, do him homage,
Subject his coronet to his crown, and bend
The dukedom, yet unbowed – alas, poor Milan! – 115
To most ignoble stooping.

MIRANDA

Oh, the heavens!

PROSPERO

Mark his condition, and th' event; then tell me
If this might be a brother.

MIRANDA

I should sin
To think but nobly of my grandmother:
Good wombs have borne bad sons.

PROSPERO

Now the condition: 120
This King of Naples, being an enemy
To me inveterate, hearkens my brother's suit;
Which was, that he, in lieu o' the premises
Of homage and I know not how much tribute,

125 **presently**   immediately, at once.

    extirpate   banish, drive out.

128 **levied**   gathered together.

129 **Fated to the purpose**   destined for this role.

131 **The ministers for the purpose**   those ordered to carry out the plan.

134 **o'er**   over.

134–5 **It is a hint . . . to 't**   the very suggestion of it makes me burst into tears.

137 **Which now's upon 's**   which is happening now.

138 **impertinent**   off the point, a diversion.

    Wherefore   why.

140 **durst**   dared.

141 **bore**   held for.

141–2 **set . . . business**   shed blood in the execution of the plot.

143 **With colours . . . foul ends**   they used fair faces to cover evil deeds. The painting metaphor may refer to the way hunters who killed a deer would be marked or painted with the animal's blood.

144 **In few**   in short.

    bark   ship.

146 **A rotten carcass of a butt**   a mere tub of a ship (like the bare bones of a dead animal).

Should presently extirpate me and mine   125
Out of the dukedom, and confer fair Milan,
With all the honours, on my brother. Whereon,
A treacherous army levied, one midnight
Fated to the purpose, did Antonio open
The gates of Milan; and, i' the dead of darkness,   130
The ministers for the purpose hurried thence
Me and thy crying self.

MIRANDA

                Alack, for pity!
I, not remembering how I cried out then,
Will cry it o'er again. It is a hint
That wrings mine eyes to 't.

PROSPERO

                Hear a little further,   135
And then I 'll bring thee to the present business
Which now 's upon 's; without the which this story
Were most impertinent.

MIRANDA

                Wherefore did they not
That hour destroy us?

PROSPERO

                Well demanded, wench.
My tale provokes that question. Dear, they
   durst not,   140
So dear the love my people bore me; nor set
A mark so bloody on the business; but
With colours fairer painted their foul ends.
In few, they hurried us aboard a bark,
Bore us some leagues to sea; where they
   prepared   145
A rotten carcass of a butt, not rigged,

27

147–8 **the very rats . . . quit it**   sea folklore has it that rats are the last to leave a sinking ship. Prospero indicates the poor quality of their ship by saying that the rats had already left it.

148 **hoist us**   left us to drift away.

150–1 **whose pity . . . loving wrong**   the winds were not as strong as the sea, they 'sighed' where the sea 'roared'. Shakespeare personifies the wind saying it felt pity, acting like a caring god.

152 **a cherubin**   a chubby-faced heavenly spirit.

153 **Thou wast . . . preserve me**   you were the one who saved me.

154 **Infuséd with . . . heaven**   with a heavenly strength.

155 **decked**   covered.

drops full salt   tears.

156 **my burthen**   burden, the weight of my troubles.

157 **undergoing stomach**   strong determination.

158 **ensue**   happen in the future.

159 **Providence divine**   the benevolent care of the gods.

161 **Neapolitan**   a citizen of Naples in Italy.

162 **charity**   Christian goodness, generosity.

162–3 **being then . . . design**   having been put in charge of this plan.

165 **steaded much**   been of great use.

166–7 **furnished me . . . volumes**   gave me books from my own collection.

168 **prize above**   value more than.

Nor tackle, sail, nor mast; the very rats
Instinctively have quit it. There they hoist us,
To cry to the sea that roared to us; to sigh
To the winds, whose pity, sighing back again,   150
Did us but loving wrong.

MIRANDA

                 Alack, what trouble
Was I then to you!

PROSPERO

              Oh, a cherubin
Thou wast that did preserve me. Thou didst smile,
Infuséd with a fortitude from heaven,
When I have decked the sea with drops full
    salt,   155
Under my burthen groaned; which raised in me
An undergoing stomach, to bear up
Against what should ensue.

MIRANDA

               How came we ashore?

PROSPERO

By Providence divine.
Some food we had, and some fresh water, that   160
A noble Neapolitan, Gonzalo,
Out of his charity, who being then appointed
Master of this design, did give us, with
Rich garments, linens, stuffs and necessaries,
Which since have steaded much. So, of his
    gentleness,   165
Knowing I loved my books, he furnished me
From mine own library with volumes that
I prize above my dukedom.

172–4 **Have I . . . so careful**   by acting as her teacher Prospero has provided a better education for her than she would have got as a princess in Milan.

176 **'t is beating in my mind**   I am very curious.

177 **Know thus far forth**   know this much.

178–9 **bountiful Fortune . . . lady**   good luck now being on my side. (Fortune is personified as a lady.)

179–80 **hath mine enemies Brought**   has brought all my enemies.

180 **prescience**   foresight.

181 **my zenith**   my highest point. In astrology every person has one time when fortune is most favourable.

182 **auspicious**   happy.

182–4 **whose influence . . . droop**   if I ignore or don't woo (the 'star') I shall from then on have worsening luck. Prospero means he must seize the moment.

184 **cease more questions**   don't ask any more questions.

185 **Thou art inclined to sleep**   you feel like sleeping. Prospero is using his magic to make her sleep.

186 **give it way**   let yourself give in to it.

187 **away**   here.

MIRANDA
                              Would I might
But ever see that man!

PROSPERO
                              Now I arise.
Sit still, and hear the last of our sea-sorrow.   170
Here in this island we arrived; and here
Have I, thy schoolmaster, made thee more profit
Than other princesses can, that have more time
For vainer hours, and tutors not so careful.

MIRANDA
Heavens thank you for 't! And now, I pray you,
     sir,   175
For still 't is beating in my mind, your reason
For raising this sea-storm.

PROSPERO
                    Know thus far forth.
By accident most strange, bountiful Fortune,
Now my dear lady, hath mine enemies
Brought to this shore; and by my prescience   180
I find my zenith doth depend upon
A most auspicious star, whose influence
If now I court not, but omit, my fortunes
Will ever after droop. Here cease more questions;
Thou art inclined to sleep. 'T is a good
     dullness,   185
And give it way. I know thou canst not choose.

                              MIRANDA *falls asleep*

Come away, servant, come. I am ready now.
Approach, my Ariel, come.

Enter ARIEL.

31

190 **To answer thy best pleasure** to fulfil your greatest desire.

be 't whether it be.

193 **quality** powers, or possibly servants.

194 **Performed . . . bade thee?** created the storm just as I told you to.

195 **article** last detail.

196 **beak** the very front of the ship, often an ornamental piece which hangs out over the sea; the prow.

197 **waist** the middle of the ship.

deck the poop-deck at the back of the ship.

198 **flamed amazement** Ariel terrorised those on board by appearing as flames.

200 **yards** the long beam on the base of the mast.

bowsprit a pole running out from the front of the ship to support the sails and their ropes.

201–3 **Jove's lightnings . . . were not** Ariel is saying that his appearance as fire was more dramatic and swift than lightning. Jove was the Roman king of the gods.

204 **Neptune** the Roman god of the sea.

205 **besiege** take up arms in battle.

206 **trident** the three-pronged fork carried by Neptune.

207 **firm, so constant** loyal and reliable.

coil uproar.

208 **infect** influence.

209 **But felt . . . mad** everyone was led to believe they were mentally ill and suffering from a fever such as 'mad' people feel.

ARIEL

    All hail, great master! Grave sir, hail! I come

    To answer thy best pleasure; be 't to fly,   190

    To swim, to dive into the fire, to ride

    On the curled clouds, to thy strong bidding task

    Ariel and all his quality.

PROSPERO

                    Has thou, spirit,

    Performed to point the tempest that I bade thee?

ARIEL

    To every article.   195

    I boarded the King's ship. Now on the beak,

    Now in the waist, the deck, in every cabin,

    I flamed amazement. Sometime I 'd divide,

    And burn in many places; on the topmast,

    The yards and bowsprit would I flame

        distinctly,   200

    Then meet and join. Jove's lightnings, the

        precursors

    O' the dreadful thunder-claps, more momentary

    And sight-outrunning were not. The fire and cracks

    Of sulphurous roaring the most mighty Neptune

    Seemed to besiege, and make his bold waves

        tremble,   205

    Yea, his dread trident shake.

PROSPERO

                  My brave spirit!

    Who was so firm, so constant, that this coil

    Would not infect his reason?

ARIEL

                  Not a soul

    But felt a fever of the mad, and played

211 *the foaming brine*   the rough sea.

    quit   left.

212 *all afire*   see note to line 198 above.

213 *up-staring*   standing up on end.

216 *nigh*   near to the.

217 *Not a hair perished*   not a hair on their heads is harmed.

218 *sustaining garments*   clothes that held them up at sea.

    blemish   mark.

219 *as thou bad'st me*   as you commanded me.

220 *In troops . . . isle*   I have scattered them in groups around the island.

223 *an odd angle*   a far corner.

224 *in this sad knot*   folded sadly like this.

225 *how thou hast disposed*   where you have put them.

Some tricks of desperation. All but mariners   210
Plunged in the foaming brine, and quit the vessel,
Then all afire with me. The King's son, Ferdinand,
With hair up-staring – then like reeds, not hair –
Was the first man that leaped; cried, 'Hell is empty,
And all the devils are here.'

PROSPERO

                    Why, that 's my spirit!   215
But was not this nigh shore?

ARIEL

               Close by, my master.

PROSPERO

But are they, Ariel, safe?

ARIEL

             Not a hair perished;
On their sustaining garments not a blemish,
But fresher than before. And, as thou bad'st me,
In troops I have dispersed them 'bout the isle.   220
The King's son have I landed by himself,
Whom I left cooling of the air with sighs
In an odd angle of the isle, and sitting
His arms in this sad knot. *(He folds his arms.)*

PROSPERO

             Of the King's ship,
The mariners, say how thou hast disposed,   225
And all the rest o' the fleet.

ARIEL

           Safely in harbour
Is the King's ship; in the deep nook, where once
Thou call'dst me up at midnight to fetch dew

229 **still-vexed Bermoothes**   the Bermudas, which were known for their storms ('vexed') and believed to be inhabited by devils.

230 **under hatches stowed**   kept inside the ship. The description makes them sound like luggage.

231–2 **Who, with a charm . . . asleep**   Ariel has used magic to make them sleep.

233 **dispersed**   separated from one another.

234 **flote**   sea.

236 **wracked**   shipwrecked.

237 **his great person perish**   the king killed.

    thy charge   your duty.

239 **Past the mid season**   after noon.

240 **At least two glasses**   by two hours at least.

    'twixt   between.

241 **spent most preciously**   used to the full.

242 **toil**   work.

    pains   hard work to perform.

244 **performed**   given to.

2454 **liberty**   freedom.

246 **be out**   is up.

From the still-vexed Bermoothes, there she 's hid;
The mariners all under hatches stowed;   230
Who, with a charm joined to their suffered labour,
I have left asleep. And for the rest o' the fleet,
Which I dispersed, they all have met again,
And are upon the Mediterranean flote,
Bound sadly home for Naples,   235
Supposing that they saw the King's ship wracked,
And his great person perish.

PROSPERO

                    Ariel, thy charge
Exactly is performed; but there 's more work.
What is the time o' the day?

ARIEL

                  Past the mid season.

PROSPERO

At least two glasses. The time 'twixt six and now   240
Must by us both be spent most preciously.

ARIEL

Is there more toil? Since thou dost give me pains,
Let me remember thee what thou hast promised,
Which is not yet performed me.

PROSPERO

                  How now, moody?
What is 't thou canst demand?

ARIEL

                  My liberty.   245

PROSPERO

Before the time be out? No more!

246 **I prithee**   I beg you.

248 **mistakings**   errors.

249 **or**   any.

250 **bate me a full year**   reduce my time as your servant by a year.

252 **think'st it much**   consider it a great chore.

255 **the veins o' th' earth**   the waters under the earth.

257 **malignant**   evil.

258 **Sycorax**   may be based on the mythological figure Circe who was exiled to an island, her crime being that she seduced men and turned them into animals.

259 **grown into a hoop**   the meaning is unclear; perhaps bent over with age.

261 **Argier**   Algiers.

ARIEL

                             I prithee,
Remember I have done thee worthy service;
Told thee no lies, made no mistakings, served
Without or grudge or grumblings. Thou did promise
To bate me a full year.

PROSPERO

                           Dost thou forget   250
From what a torment I did free thee?

ARIEL

                     No.

PROSPERO

Thou dost, and think'st it much to tread the ooze
Of the salt deep,
To run upon the sharp wind of the north,
To do me business in the veins o' th' earth   255
When it is baked with frost.

ARIEL

                I do not, sir.

PROSPERO

Thou liest, malignant thing! Hast thou forgot
The foul witch Sycorax, who with age and envy
Was grown into a hoop? Hast thou forgot her?

ARIEL

No, sir.

PROSPERO

            Thou hast. Where was she born? Speak.
Tell me.   260

ARIEL

Sir, in Argier.

264 **mischiefs manifold**   her many acts of wickedness.

   sorceries   magic spells.

266 **banished**   sent to live in exile.

266–7 **For one thing . . . life**   either, because of an unexplained incident, or, because she was pregnant.

271 **As thou report'st thyself**   as you yourself told me.

272 **for thou wast**   because you were.

273 **abhorred**   much hated, appalling.

274 **grand hests**   great requests.

   confine thee   imprison you.

275 **more potent ministers**   stronger agents or servants.

276 **most unmitigable rage**   strongest anger which could not be reduced.

277 **cloven**   split.

280 **vent thy groans**   cry out loud.

281 **strike**   turn.

282 **litter**   give birth to; usually used when speaking of an animal.

283 **whelp**   an insulting term for a boy, like the young of an animal.

PROSPERO

          Oh, was she so? I must
Once in a month recount what thou hast been,
Which thou forget'st. This damned witch Sycorax,
For mischiefs manifold, and sorceries terrible
To enter human hearing, from Argier,   265
Thou know'st, was banished. For one thing she
    did
They would not take her life. Is not this true?

ARIEL

    Ay, sir.

PROSPERO

This blue-eyed hag was hither brought with child,
And here was left by the sailors. Thou, my slave, 270
As thou report'st thyself, wast then her servant;
And, for thou wast a spirit too delicate
To act her earthy and abhorred commands,
Refusing her grand hests, she did confine thee,
By help of her more potent ministers,   275
And in her most unmitigable rage,
Into a cloven pine; within which rift
Imprisoned thou didst painfully remain
A dozen years; within which space she died,
And left thee there; where thou didst vent thy
    groans   280
As fast as mill-wheels strike. Then was this island –
Save for the son that she did litter here,
A freckled whelp hag-born – not honoured with
A human shape.

ARIEL

          Yes, Caliban her son.

286 *in service* as a servant.

291 *Art* good magic powers.

292 *gape* open up.

294 *murmur'st* complains.

    rend tear apart.

295 *peg thee* inprison you.

297 *correspondent* willingly obedient.

299 *discharge thee* set you free.

301 *nymph* beautiful young woman.

302–3 *Be subject . . . mine* be invisible to all but you and me.

PROSPERO

Dull thing, I say so; he, that Caliban,   285
Whom now I keep in service. Thou best know'st
What torment I did find thee in; thy groans
Did make wolves howl, and penetrate the breasts
Of ever-angry bears. It was a torment
To lay upon the damned, which Sycorax   290
Could not again undo. It was mine Art,
When I arrived and heard thee, that made gape
The pine, and let thee out.

ARIEL

I thank thee, master.

PROSPERO

If thou more murmur'st, I will rend an oak,
And peg thee in his knotty entrails, till   295
Thou hast howled away twelve winters.

ARIEL

Pardon, master.
I will be correspondent to command,
And do my spiriting gently.

PROSPERO

Do so; and after two days
I will discharge thee.

ARIEL

That 's my noble master!
What shall I do? Say what! What shall I do?   300

PROSPERO

Go make thyself like a nymph o' the sea:
Be subject to
No sight but thine and mine; invisible
To every eyeball else. Go take this shape,

306   **diligence**   hard work.

308–9   **put Heaviness in me**   made me drowsy.

311   **Yields us**   willingly gives us a.

313   **miss**   manage without.

314   **serves in offices**   does jobs.

315   **profit**   help.

316   **Thou earth**   being Sycorax's child Caliban is of the earth in contrast to Ariel who is of the air.

   within   inside.

317   **forth**   out here.

   There's other . . . thee   I have another task for you.

318   **tortoise**   Caliban moves slowly.

And hither come in 't. Go, hence,   305
With diligence.

Exit ARIEL

(*To* MIRANDA) Awake, dear heart, awake! Thou hast
    slept well.

Awake!

MIRANDA
            The strangeness of your story put
Heaviness in me.

PROSPERO
            Shake it off. Come on;
We 'll visit Caliban my slave, who never   310
Yields us kind answer.

MIRANDA
                        'T is a villain, sir,
I do not love to look on.

PROSPERO
                        But, as 't is,
We cannot miss him. He does make our fire,
Fetch in our wood, and serves in offices
That profit us. What, ho! slave! Caliban!   315
Thou earth, thou, speak!

CALIBAN
            (*Within*) There 's wood enough within.

PROSPERO
Come forth, I say! There 's other business for thee.
Come, thou tortoise! When?

Enter ARIEL *like a water-nymph.*

45

319 **Fine apparition**   wonderful vision.

320 **Hark in thine ear**   listen.

321 **got by the devil himself**   Caliban was born of a union between Sycorax (a witch) and a devil.

322 **dam**   mother (usually of animals).

323–6 **As wicked . . . you all o'er**   Caliban issues a curse on Prospero and Miranda.

328 **pen thy breath up**   make you lose your breath.

   urchins   hedgehogs.

329 **that vast of night**   all through the long night.

333 **by**   as inherited by right from.

337 **the bigger light**   the sun.

   the less   the moon.

Fine apparition! My quaint Ariel,
Hark in thine ear. *(He whispers instructions to* ARIEL.*)*

ARIEL

           My lord, it shall be done.   320

                                             Exit

PROSPERO

Thou poisonous slave, got by the devil himself
Upon thy wicked dam, come forth!

Enter CALIBAN.

CALIBAN

As wicked dew as e'er my mother brushed
With raven's feather from unwholesome fen
Drop on you both! A south-west blow on ye   325
And blister you all o'er!

PROSPERO

For this, be sure, tonight thou shalt have cramps,
Side-stitches that shall pen thy breath up; urchins
Shall, for that vast of night that they may work,
All exercise on thee; thou shalt be pinched   330
As thick as honeycomb, each pinch more stinging
Than bees that made 'em.

CALIBAN

                   I must eat my dinner.
This island 's mine, by Sycorax my mother,
Which thou tak'st from me. When thou cam'st
    first,
Thou strok'st me, and made much of me;
    wouldst give me   335
Water with berries in 't; and teach me how
To name the bigger light, and how the less,

339 **qualities**   natural beauties.

340 **The fresh springs . . . fertile**   he showed them what was good and bad, such as fresh water and salt water, so that they would know which to use.

341 **Cursed . . . did so**   may I be cursed for doing so.

charms   spells.

343 **subjects**   servants, king's followers.

344 **Which first . . . king**   when at first I was the king.

sty me   make me live in a sty, as an animal.

347 **stripes may move**   the lash of a whip has an effect on him.

348 **lodged thee**   let you live.

349–50 **violate The honour**   ruin the purity (Caliban tried to rape Miranda).

351 **Would't**   I wish it.

352–3 **I had peopled . . . Calibans**   otherwise I would have produced many of my own offspring for the island.

353 **Abhorréd**   hateful.

354 **Which any . . . not take**   teaching about goodness made no impression on Caliban.

357–8 **didst not . . . meaning**   didn't even understand your own thoughts.

359–60 **I endowed . . . them known**   I taught you how to use words to express your thoughts.

360 **race**   Caliban's inherited characteristics were such that.

That burn by day and night. And then I loved thee,
And showed thee all the qualities o' th' isle,
The fresh springs, brine-pits, barren place and
    fertile.   340
Cursed be I that did so! All the charms
Of Sycorax, toads, beetles, bats, light on you!
For I am all the subjects that you have,
Which first was mine own king! And here you
    sty me
In this hard rock, whiles you do keep from me   345
The rest o' th' island.

PROSPERO
               Thou most lying slave,
Whom stripes may move, not kindness! I have
    used thee,
Filth as thou art, with human care, and lodged thee
In mine own cell, till thou didst seek to violate
The honour of my child.   350

CALIBAN
Oh ho! Oh ho! Would 't had been done!
Thou didst prevent me; I had peopled else
This isle with Calibans.

PROSPERO
              Abhorréd slave,
Which any print of goodness wilt not take,
Being capable of all ill! I pitied thee,   355
Took pains to make thee speak, taught thee
    each hour
One thing or other. When thou didst not, savage,
Know thine own meaning, but wouldst gabble like
A thing most brutish, I endowed thy purposes
With words that made them known. But thy vile
    race,   360

363 **confined into** kept in the boundaries of.

364 **more** worse.

365 **my profit on't** how it has helped me.

366–7 **The red plague . . . learning me** may you die by the plague as a reward for teaching me.

367 **Hag-seed** the produce of a witch ('hag').

hence go away.

368–9 **thou'rt best . . . business** you had better do you work.

371 **I'll rack . . . cramps** I will fill your body with pains as if you were on the rack (an instrument of torture).

373 **That** so that.

thy din the noise you make.

'pray thee I beg you.

375–6 **control . . . vassal of him** even my mother's god (or, the devil himself) would be turned into a willing servant (by this pain).

380 **whist** quietened.

Though thou didst learn, had that in 't which
   good natures
Could not abide to be with. Therefore wast thou
Deservedly confined into this rock,
Who hadst deserved more than a prison.

CALIBAN
You taught me language; and my profit on 't   365
Is, I know how to curse. The red plague rid you
For learning me your language!

PROSPERO
               Hag-seed, hence!
Fetch us in fuel; and be quick, thou 'rt best,
To answer other business. Shrug'st thou, malice?
If thou neglect'st, or dost unwillingly   370
What I command, I 'll rack thee with old cramps,
Fill all thy bones with aches, make thee roar,
That beasts shall tremble at thy din.

CALIBAN
               No, 'pray thee.
(Aside) I must obey. His Art is of such pow'r,
It would control my dam's god, Setebos,   375
And make a vassal of him.

PROSPERO
             So, slave; hence!
                       Exit CALIBAN

Enter FERDINAND *led by* ARIEL, *invisible, playing and singing.*

ARIEL'S *song*
    Come unto these yellow sands
      And then take hands.
    Courtsied when you have and kissed,
      The wild waves whist,   380

381 *Foot it featly*   walk daintily.

383 **burthen**   burden or refrain in a song.

391 *waits upon*   is played to please.

393 *wrack*   shipwreck.

395 *Allaying*   making quiet; calming.

396 *Thence*   from there.

399 *Full fathom five*   five fathoms deep (in the sea).

403 *sea-change*   completely changed by the sea. The description makes it
         appear that he has been dead for a long time.

408 *ditty*   words of the song.

       remember   remind me of.

Foot it featly here and there,
  And sweet sprites bear
The burthen. Hark, hark.
(Burthen dispersedly:) *Bow-wow.*
The watch dogs bark.   385
(Burthen dispersedly:) *Bow-wow.*
Hark, hark! I hear
The strain of strutting chanticleer
Cry – Cock a diddle dow.

FERDINAND

Where should this music be? I' th' air or
    th' earth?   390
It sounds no more; and, sure, it waits upon
Some god o' th' island. Sitting on a bank,
Weeping again the King my father's wrack,
This music crept by me upon the waters,
Allaying both their fury and my passion   395
With its sweet air. Thence I have follow'd it,
Or it hath drawn me rather. But 't is gone.
No, it begins again.

ARIEL'S *song*

Full fathom five thy father lies;
  Of his bones are coral made;   400
Those are pearls that were his eyes.
  Nothing of him that doth fade,
But doth suffer a sea-change
Into something rich and strange.
Sea-nymphs hourly ring his knell.   405
    (Burthen:) *Ding-dong.*
Hark! Now I hear them - Ding-dong, bell.

FERDINAND

The ditty does remember my drowned father.

409 **This is no mortal business**   this is not produced by humans. Ferdinand believes he is hearing heavenly music.

410 **That the earth owes**   that belongs to the earth.

411 **The fringéd . . . advance**   open your eyes.

412 **yond**   over there.

414 **brave**   excellent, handsome.

416 **gallant**   gentleman.

417–8 **but he's . . . grief**   apart from the fact that he is grieving.

418 **canker**   cancer, or destroyer.

422–3 **It goes on . . . prompts it**   my plan is working as I intended.

424–5 **Most sure . . . airs attend**   Ferdinand has seen Miranda and assumes she is the goddess for whom the music has been played.

This is no mortal business, nor no sound
That the earth owes. – I hear it now above me.   410

PROSPERO

   (To MIRANDA*)* The fringéd curtains of thine eye
     advance,
And say what thou seest yond.

MIRANDA

                    What is 't? A spirit?
Lord, how it looks about! Believe me, sir,
It carries a brave form. But 't is a spirit.

PROSPERO

No, wench; it eats and sleeps and hath such
     senses   415
As we have, such. This gallant which thou seest
Was in the wrack; and, but he 's something stained
With grief (that 's beauty's canker), thou mightst
     call him
A goodly person. He hath lost his fellows,
And strays about to find 'em.

MIRANDA

                 I might call him   420
A thing divine, for nothing natural
I ever saw so noble.

PROSPERO

             (Aside) It goes on, I see,
As my soul prompts it. *(To* ARIEL*)* Spirit, fine spirit!
     I 'll free thee
Within two days for this.

FERDINAND

             Most sure the goddess

425 **Vouchsafe**   accept.

428 **bear me**   conduct myself.

   prime request   main question.

430 **maid**   still unmarried.

432 **the best of them that**   the noblest of men to.

433 **Were I but where 't is spoken**   Ferdinand wishes he was at his home as
   there he would be seen as the nobleman that he is.

   How   how is it that you are.

434 **wert thou**   would you be.

435 **A single thing**   alone.

   wonders   is amazed.

436 **He does hear me**   now that Ferdinand thinks his father is dead he believes
   himself to be the king of Naples. Thus he hears himself speak, or perhaps
   thinks his father's spirit hears him.

437 **Naples**   the king of Naples.

438 **ne'er since . . . beheld**   which haven't stopped crying since I saw.

441 **Duke of Milan**   here Prospero means himself, the rightful duke of Milan.

On whom these airs attend! Vouchsafe my
    prayer   425
May know if you remain upon this island;
And that you will some good instruction give
How I may bear me here. My prime request,
Which I do last pronounce, is – Oh, you wonder! –
If you be maid or no?

MIRANDA

                     No wonder, sir;   430
But certainly a maid.

FERDINAND

                My language! heavens!
I am the best of them that speak this speech,
Were I but where 't is spoken.

PROSPERO

                  How, the best?
What wert thou, if the King of Naples heard thee?

FERDINAND

A single thing, as I am now, that wonders   435
To hear thee speak of Naples. He does hear me;
And that he does I weep. Myself am Naples,
Who with mine eyes, ne'er since at ebb, beheld
The King my father wracked.

MIRANDA

                Alack, for mercy!

FERDINAND

Yes, faith, and all his lords; the Duke of Milan   440
And his brave son being twain.

PROSPERO

                (Aside) The Duke of Milan

442 **control thee**   prove you wrong.

443 **fit**   the right time.

444 **changed eyes**   fallen in love.

448 **third man**   i.e. Prospero, Caliban and Ferdinand being the only three men she has seen.

e'er I   I ever.

450 **To be inclined my way!**   to see things from my point of view.

451 **And your affection not gone forth**   and not promised to someone else; in love with someone else.

453 **both in either's powers**   totally wrapped up in each other.

454 **uneasy**   difficult.

light   easy.

455 **light**   of less value.

456 **attend**   listen to.

456–7 **usurp . . . ow'st not**   steal a name which doesn't belong to you. This is in fact true as Ferdinand's father, the king of Naples, is not dead.

459 **as I am a man**   he swears by his manhood.

460 **There's nothing ill . . . temple**   Miranda refers to the body as a temple, believing that such a handsome outer appearance must mean that Ferdinand is honest.

And his more braver daughter could control thee,
If now 't were fit to do 't. At the first sight
They have changed eyes. Delicate Ariel,
I 'll set thee free for this. *(To* FERDINAND) A word,
    good sir;   445
I fear you have done yourself some wrong. A word.

MIRANDA

    (Aside) Why speaks my father so ungently? This
    Is the third man that e'er I saw; the first
    That e'er I sighed for. Pity move my father
    To be inclined my way!

FERDINAND

                      (Aside) Oh, if a virgin,   450
    And your affection not gone forth, I 'll make you
    The Queen of Naples.

PROSPERO

                Soft, sir! One word more.
    (Aside) They are both in either's powers. But this
        swift business
    I must uneasy make, lest too light winning
    Make the prize light. *(To* FERDINAND) One word
        more; I charge thee   455
    That thou attend me. Thou dost here usurp
    The name thou ow'st not; and hast put thyself
    Upon this island as a spy, to win it
    From me, the lord on 't.

FERDINAND

                No, as I am a man.

MIRANDA

    (Aside) There 's nothing ill can dwell in such
        a temple.   460

461 *a house*   i.e. Ferdinand's body.

462 *strive*   try.

 dwell   live.

466 *fresh-brook*   fresh water.

468 *entertainment*   treatment, behaviour.

471 *gentle, and not fearful*   a nobleman, not a coward.

472 *My foot my tutor?*   do you think you can teach me? As Prospero's daughter, Miranda is merely a lowly part of Prospero.

 Put thy sword up   put your sword away.

473 *mak'st a show . . . strike*   puts on a show but hasn't the guts to attack.

474 *Come from thy ward*   this refers to a fencing term, he is telling him to lower his guard.

475 *stick*   magic staff.

If the ill spirit have so fair a house,
Good things will strive to dwell with 't.

PROSPERO

(To FERDINAND*)* Follow me!
(To MIRANDA*)* Speak not you for him; he's a traitor.
(To FERDINAND*)* Come!
I 'll manacle thy neck and feet together;
Sea-water shalt thou drink; thy food shall be   465
The fresh-brook mussels, withered roots, and
    husks
Wherein the acorn cradled. Follow!

FERDINAND

No!
I will resist such entertainment till
Mine enemy has more power.

*(He draws his sword but is prevented from moving by
Prospero's magic power.)*

MIRANDA

O dear father,
Make not too rash a trial of him, for   470
He 's gentle, and not fearful.

PROSPERO

What! I say,
My foot my tutor? *(To* FERDINAND*)* Put thy sword
    up, traitor;
Who mak'st a show, but dar'st not strike, thy
    conscience
Is so possessed with guilt. Come from thy ward;
For I can here disarm thee with this stick   475
And make thy weapon drop.

478 **surety**   guarantee.

479 **chide**   tell you off.

480 **An advocate for an imposter!**   will you defend a liar?

481 **no more such shapes as he**   no other man who looks like him.

482 **but**   only.

483 **To**   in comparison to.

486 **goodlier**   better.

487 **Thy nerves . . . again**   your muscles are as weak as a baby's.

488 **vigour**   strength.

489 **spirits**   feelings.

491 **The wrack . . . friends**   all my friends being shipwrecked.

491–4 **nor this man's threats . . . maid**   Ferdinand states that none of these things
would be too much to bear if he could just see Miranda each day.

MIRANDA

Beseech you, father.

PROSPERO

Hence! hang not on my garments.

MIRANDA

Sir, have pity.

I 'll be his surety.

PROSPERO

Silence! One word more
Shall make me chide thee, if not hate thee. What!
An advocate for an impostor! Hush!   480
Thou think'st there is no more such shapes as he,
Having seen but him and Caliban. Foolish wench!
To the most of men this is a Caliban,
And they to him are angels.

MIRANDA

My affections
Are then most humble; I have no ambition   485
To see a goodlier man.

PROSPERO

(*To* FERDINAND) Come on; obey.
Thy nerves are in their infancy again,
And have no vigour in them.

FERDINAND

So they are.
My spirits, as in a dream, are all bound up.
My father's loss, the weakness which I feel,   490
The wrack of all my friends, nor this man's threats,
To whom I am subdued, are but light to me,
Might I but through my prison once a day

494–5 **All corners . . . use of**   I do not need to make use of the wide world – let free men have it.

496 **It works**   the plan is working. Prospero's intention was that separating Miranda and Ferdinand would make Ferdinand love her more.

498 **what thou . . . do me**   what else you shall do for me.

500 **unwonted**   unusual.

502 **But then**   only.

Behold this maid. All corners else o' th' earth
Let liberty make use of; space enough   495
Have I in such a prison.

PROSPERO

      (Aside) It works. *(To* FERDINAND*)* Come on.
(To ARIEL*)* Thou hast done well, fine Ariel!
                  (To FERDINAND*)* Follow me.
(To ARIEL*)* Hark what thou else shalt do me.

MIRANDA

          (To FERDINAND*)* Be of comfort;
My father 's of a better nature, sir,
Than he appears by speech. This is unwonted   500
Which now came from him.

PROSPERO

         (To ARIEL*)* Thou shalt be as free
As mountain winds. But then exactly do
All points of my command.

ARIEL

          To the syllable.

PROSPERO

Come, follow. *(To* MIRANDA*)* Speak not for him.

                           Exeunt

Christopher Benjamin as Stephano and Bob Peck as Caliban: Royal Shakespeare Company, 1982.

Act 2: summary

The action moves to another part of the island where Alonso, king of Naples, and his men are shipwrecked. Alonso cannot be comforted as he believes his son, Ferdinand, is dead. Gonzalo tries to raise the King's spirits by talking about the island and the potential for its development as a commonwealth. Sebastian, the King's brother, and Antonio, Prospero's brother, mock Gonzalo for his age and dull speech.

Ariel enters and makes them all sleep except Sebastian and Antonio. Antonio persuades Sebastian to kill Alonso, so that Sebastian can be king, but just as they are about to do this Ariel makes the others wake up.

Back at Prospero's cell, Caliban is carrying wood and complaining when Trinculo, Alonso's jester, appears. Caliban hides under a cloak and Trinculo makes jokes about this strange island creature he has found. A thunderstorm begins and Trinculo decides to shelter under Caliban's cloak. Then Stephano, Alonso's butler, appears. He is drunk and singing a sea-shanty. Seeing the cloak with Caliban and Trinculo under it Stephano believes he has found a creature with four legs. Caliban thinks Stephano is a spirit sent by Prospero to punish him and cries out in terror. Stephano speaks to Caliban and gives him wine, and hearing Stephano's voice, which he recognises, Trinculo thinks this is the work of devils. Stephano hears Trinculo's voice and thinks the monster has two mouths as well as four legs. Trinculo then realises it is Stephano, calls to him and Stephano thinks it is a devil who knows his name.

Trinculo identifies himself, and they celebrate the fact that they have both survived the storm. Caliban assumes they must be gods and kneels before them, promising to serve them and show them the riches of the island. He is celebrating too, as he believes these new masters will free him from Prospero's rule.

I **Beseech you**   I beg you.

3 **hint of woe**   sad experience.

6 **theme**   experience.

but for   it is only due to.

9 **Prithee, peace**   please be quiet.

10 **He receives . . . porridge**   the phrase shows Sebastian joking at Gonzalo and Alonso's expense. He and Antonio continue to do so throughout the scene.

11 **The visitor**   one who visited to give comfort.

give him o'er   abandon him.

12–13 **winding up . . . strike**   Sebastian suggests Gonzalo speaks without great wisdom or intelligence.

Act Two

Scene one

Another part of the island.

Enter ALONSO, SEBASTIAN, ANTONIO, GONZALO, ADRIAN, FRANCISCO, *and others.*

GONZALO

    (To ALONSO*)* Beseech you, sir, be merry; you have
        cause,
    So have we all, of joy; for our escape
    Is much beyond our loss. Our hint of woe
    Is common; every day, some sailor's wife,
    The masters of some merchant, and the
        merchant,   5
    Have just our theme of woe; but for the miracle,
    I mean our preservation, few in millions
    Can speak like us. Then wisely, good sir, weigh
    Our sorrow with our comfort.

ALONSO

    Prithee, peace!

SEBASTIAN

    (Aside to ANTONIO*)* He receives comfort like cold
        porridge.   10

ANTONIO

    (To SEBASTIAN*)* The visitor will not give him o'er so.

SEBASTIAN

    Look, he 's winding up the watch of his wit; by and
    by it will strike.

15 *One* the first strike of the clock.

    tell keep count.

16 *entertained* received.

17 *th' entertainer* the one who receives it.

18 *A dollar* i.e. payment.

19 *Dolour* grief, pain; pun on the word in the previous line.

20 *purposed* realised.

21 *wiselier* to mean something wiser.

23 *spendthrift . . . his tongue* Antonio mocks Gonzalo for having few words, spending language like a miser spends money.

24 *spare* give no more.

27 *Adrian* the young cock.

27–8 *for a good wager . . . to crow* Sebastian and Antonio make a bet about who will speak first, Adrian (being young he is 'the cockerel') or Gonzalo ('the old cock').

GONZALO
    Sir –

SEBASTIAN
    One; tell.   15

GONZALO
    When every grief is entertained that 's offered,
    Comes to th' entertainer –

SEBASTIAN
    A dollar.

GONZALO
    Dolour comes to him, indeed: you have spoken
    truer than you purposed.   20

SEBASTIAN
    You have taken it wiselier than I meant you should.

GONZALO
    (To ALONSO) Therefore, my lord –

ANTONIO
    Fie, what a spendthrift is he of his tongue!

ALSONSO
    I prithee, spare.

GONZALO
    Well, I have done. But yet –   25

SEBASTIAN
    He will be talking.

ANTONIO
    Which, of he or Adrian, for a good wager, first
    begins to crow?

SEBASTIAN
    The old cock.

32 **A *laughter***   the winner of the bet laughs.

33 **A *match***   the bet is set then.

38 **Yet**   Sebastian mimics Adrian by predicting his words.

41 ***temperance***   climate.

42 ***Temperance . . . wench***   Antonio mocks Adrian by taking Temperance to be a woman ('wench'). The name, meaning self-controlled and modest, was given to Puritan women because of its Biblical link.

ANTONIO
  The cockerel.   30

SEBASTIAN
  Done. The wager?

ANTONIO
  A laughter.

SEBASTIAN
  A match!

ADRIAN
  Though this island seem to be desert –

ANTONIO
  Ha, ha, ha!   35

SEBASTIAN
  So; you 're paid.

ADRIAN
  Uninhabitable, and almost inaccessible –

SEBASTIAN
  Yet –

ADRIAN
  Yet –

ANTONIO
  He could not miss 't.   40

ADRIAN
  It must needs be of subtle, tender and delicate
  temperance.

ANTONIO
  Temperance was a delicate wench.

43 **subtle**   crafty.

most learnedly delivered   Adrian's language is pompous and Sebastian
  mocks it.

45 **As if it . . . rotten ones**   Sebastian's words mean it is impossible to take
  Adrian's words seriously. He destroys the gentle image given by Adrian
  with the image of unhealthy lungs.

48 **save**   except for the.

SEBASTIAN

Ay, and a subtle, as he most learnedly delivered.

ADRIAN

The air breathes upon us here most sweetly.

SEBASTIAN

As if it had lungs, and rotten ones.   45

ANTONIO

Or as 't were perfumed by a fen.

GONZALO

Here is everything advantageous to life.

ANTONIO

True; save means to live.

SEBASTIAN

Of that there 's none, or little.

GONZALO

How lush and lusty the grass looks! How green!   50

ANTONIO

The ground, indeed, is tawny.

SEBASTIAN

With an eye of green in 't.

ANTONIO

He misses not much.

SEBASTIAN

No; he doth but mistake the truth totally.

GONZALO

But the rarity of it is – which is indeed almost   55
beyond credit –

57   **vouched**   so called.

59   **hold, notwithstanding**   still maintain.

60   **glosses**   fair appearance.

    being rather   looking more as if.

64   **pocket up**   hide.

66   **Afric**   Africa.

69–70   **'T was . . . our return**   Sebastian is clearly being sarcastic about the return journey, and, we presume, also about the marriage.

72   **to**   as.

73   **Dido's**   the queen of Carthage during the Trojan Wars; she was Sychaeus' widow.

74   **Widow**   here Antonio and Sebastian are seen ridiculing the famous and great.

SEBASTIAN

As many vouched rarities are –

GONZALO

That our garments, being, as they were, drenched
in the sea, hold, notwithstanding, their freshness
and glosses, being rather new-dyed than stained   60
with salt water.

ANTONIO

If but one of his pockets could speak, would it
not say he lies?

SEBASTIAN

Ay, or very falsely pocket up his report.

GONZALO

Methinks our garments are now as fresh as   65
when we put them on first in Afric, at the
marriage of the King's fair daughter Claribel to
the King of Tunis.

SEBASTIAN

'T was a sweet marriage, and we prosper well in
our return.   70

ADRIAN

Tunis was never graced before with such a
paragon to their Queen.

GONZALO

Not since widow Dido's time.

ANTONIO

Widow! A pox o' that! How came that widow in?
Widow Dido!   75

76 **Aeneas**   Dido's lover and then husband. This reference to them as widow
and widower seems inappropriate because they did not behave as
though they were grieving.

80 **This Tunis . . . Carthage**   Gonzalo suggests that Tunis is built on the ruins of
Carthage.

83 **His word is more . . . harp**   this refers to the Greek legend in which the
walls of Thebes built themselves up when a god played the harp. In
stating categorically that Carthage is beneath Tunis, Gonzalo has 'built'
the whole city of Carthage with ease.

87 **give it . . . an apple**   make a gift of it as if it were an apple. Sebastian is
mocking Gonzalo for so easily 'moving' Carthage.

88 **kernels**   pips.

SEBASTIAN

What if he had said 'widower Aeneas' too? Good
Lord, how you take it!

ADRIAN

'Widow Dido' said you? You make me study of that.
She was of Carthage, not of Tunis.

GONZALO

This Tunis, sir, was Carthage.   80

ADRIAN

Carthage?

GONZALO

I assure you, Carthage.

ANTONIO

His word is more than the miraculous harp.

SEBASTIAN

He hath raised the wall, and houses too.

ANTONIO

What impossible matter will he make easy next?   85

SEBASTIAN

I think he will carry this island home in his pocket,
and give it his son for an apple.

ANTONIO

And, sowing the kernels of it in the sea, bring
forth more islands

GONZALO

Ay.   90

ANTONIO

Why, in good time.

96 **Bate . . . Dido** don't forget about Dido.

99 **in a sort** up to a point.

100 **That sort was well fished for** Antonio mocks Gonzalo for qualifying the statement.

102–3 **against . . . of my sense** that I have no appetite for. He does not wish to hear them.

103 **Would I** I wish I.

104 **thence** from there.

105 **in my rate** it is my belief that.

107 **heir** he is referring to his son, Ferdinand.

108–9 **what strange fish . . . on thee** Alonso believes Ferdinand to be drowned and being eaten by fish just as Ferdinand believes Alonso to be drowned.

110 **beat the surges under him** beat down the waves.

GONZALO

    (To ALONSO*)* Sir, we were talking that our garments
    seem now as fresh as when we were at Tunis at the
    marriage of your daughter, who is now Queen.

ANTONIO

    And the rarest that e'er came there.   95

SEBASTIAN

    Bate, I beseech you, widow Dido.

ANTONIO

    Oh, widow Dido! ay, widow Dido.

GONZALO

    Is not, sir, my doublet as fresh as the first day I
    wore it? I mean, in a sort.

ANTONIO

    That sort was well fished for.   100

GONZALO

    When I wore it at your daughter's marriage?

ALONSO

    You cram these words into mine ears against
    The stomach of my sense. Would I had never
    Married my daughter there! For, coming thence,
    My son is lost, and, in my rate, she too,   105
    Who is so far from Italy removed
    I ne'er again shall see her. O thou mine heir
    Of Naples and of Milan, what strange fish
    Hath made his meal on thee?

FRANCISCO

                Sir, he may live.
    I saw him beat the surges under him,   110
    And ride upon their backs; he trod the water,

112 **Whose emnity . . . aside**   not letting the sea be his enemy.

113 **surge most swoln**   the swelling waves.

114 **'Bove**   above.

114–5 **oared Himself**   swam using his arms like oars.

115 **lusty**   healthy.

116–7 **To the shore . . . relieve him**   the foundation of the cliffs bends over to meet him and bring him safely into shore.

121 **loose**   lose.

123 **Who hath . . . on 't**   who had good reason to cry.

Prithee, peace   I beg you to be quiet.

124 **kneeled**   begged.

importuned   urged to do.

125–6 **the fair soul . . . obedience**   caught between the desire to obey and the desire not to marry.

129 **Mo**   more.

131 **So is . . . loss**   so my loss is also the greatest.

Whose enmity he flung aside, and breasted
The surge most swoln that met him; his bold head
'Bove the contentious waves he kept, and oared
Himself with his good arms in lusty stroke   115
To the shore, that o'er his wave-worn basis bowed,
As stooping to relieve him. I not doubt
He came alive to land.

ALONSO

     No, no, he 's gone.

SEBASTIAN

Sir, you may thank *yourself* for this great loss,
That would not bless our Europe with your
  daughter,   120
But rather loose her to an African;
Where she, at least, is banished from your eye,
Who hath cause to wet the grief on 't.

ALONSO

     Prithee, peace.

SEBASTIAN

You were kneeled to, and importuned otherwise,
By all of us; and the fair soul herself   125
Weighed between loathness and obedience, at
Which end o' the beam should bow. We have lost
  your son,
I fear, for ever. Milan and Naples have
Mo widows in them of this business' making
Than we bring men to comfort them.   130
The fault 's your own.

ALONSO

    So is the dear'st o' the loss.

133 **gentleness**   tact.

134 *And time to speak it in*   a good sense of timing.

136 **chirurgeonly**   like a surgeon.

137–8 *It is foul . . . cloudy*   Gonzalo uses a metaphor likening bad or sorrowful moods to poor weather which affects them all.

138 *Fowl*   like a wildfowl or duck.

139 **plantation of this isle**   the chance to colonise this island.

140 *He 'd sow . . . nettle-seed*   Antonio's comment (and that made earlier by Sebastian) shows he deliberately misunderstands Gonzalo's meaning, taking it as 'the chance to plant on'. They suggest he would plant weeds.

142 *'Scape*   escape.

143 *I' the commonwealth*   in the country where all society is equal.

143–4 *by contraries . . . all things*   behave differently from normal.

144 **traffic**   trading.

GONZALO

    My lord Sebastian,
    The truth you speak doth lack some gentleness,
    And time to speak it in. You rub the sore,
    When you should bring the plaster.

SEBASTIAN

                    Very well.   135

ANTONIO

    And most chirurgeonly.

GONZALO

    (*To* ALONSO) It is foul weather in us all, good sir,
    When you are cloudy.

SEBASTIAN

                Fowl weather?

ANTONIO

                     Very foul.

GONZALO

    Had I plantation of this isle, my lord –

ANTONIO

    He 'd sow 't with nettle-seed.

SEBASTIAN

            Or docks, or mallows.   140

GONZALO

    And were the king on 't, what would I do?

SEBASTIAN

    'Scape being drunk for want of wine.

GONZALO

    I' the commonwealth I would by contraries
    Execute all things; for no kind of traffic

145 **admit** allow.

    name title.

146 **Letters** education.

147 **service** servants.

    contract betrothal.

    succession inheritance of land, wealth or title.

148 **Bourn** boundary.

    tilth cultivation.

150 **occupation** work.

152 **sovereignty** king or queen.

152–3 **Yet he . . . the beginning** Sebastian and Antonio point out the lack of logic
    of having no king and yet being the king.

154 **common** equal.

155 **endeavour** hard work.

    treason going against the king.

    felony crime.

156–7 **Sword, pike . . . not have** I would have no need of any type of weapon.

158 **foison** full harvest.

160–1 **No marrying . . . knaves** Sebastian and Antonio again point out the lack of
    logic in Gonzalo's dream.

163 **the Golden Age** a past time when life was supposed to have been simple
    and perfect.

    'Save God save.

Would I admit; no name of magistrate;   145
Letters should not be known; riches, poverty,
And use of service, none; contract, succession,
Bourn, bound of land, tilth, vineyard, none;
No use of metal, corn, or wine, or oil;
No occupation; all men idle, all;   150
And women too, but innocent and pure;
No sovereignty –

SEBASTIAN

                  Yet he would be king on 't.

ANTONIO

  The latter end of his commonwealth forgets
    the beginning.

GONZALO

  All things in common Nature should produce
  Without sweat or endeavour; treason, felony,   155
  Sword, pike, knife, gun, or need of any engine,
  Would I not have; but Nature should bring forth,
  Of it own kind, all foison, all abundance,
  To feed my innocent people.

SEBASTIAN

  No marrying 'mong his subjects?   160

ANTONIO

  None, man; all idle; whores and knaves.

GONZALO

  I would with such perfection govern, sir,
  T' excel the Golden Age.

SEBASTIAN

                 'Save his Majesty!

164 *mark*   hear, note.

165 *nothing*   of nothing, nonsense.

167 *minister . . . gentlemen*   give these gentlemen an opportunity to make fun.

168 *sensible*   sensitive.

171 *am nothing*   mean nothing.

172–5 *So you may . . . fallen flat-long*   Gonzalo attempts to put Antonio and Sebastian in their place but they out-wit him.

176 *mettle*   substance.

176–8 *you would lift . . . without changing*   Gonzalo implies that they would take anything as a target for wit, even the moon.

179 *bat-fowling*   catching birds at night, using torches and nets. Also Elizabethan slang meaning to victimise a simple-minded person (i.e. Gonzalo).

ANTONIO

Long live Gonzalo!

GONZALO

And – do you mark me, sir?

ALONSO

Prithee, no more. Thou dost talk nothing to me. 165

GONZALO

I do well believe your highness; and did it to minister occasion to these gentlemen, who are of such sensible and nimble lungs that they always use to laugh at nothing.

ANTONIO

'T was you we laughed at. 170

GONZALO

Who in this kind of merry fooling am nothing to you. So you may continue, and laugh at nothing still.

ANTONIO

What a blow was there given!

SEBASTIAN

An it had not fallen flat-long. 175

GONZALO

You are gentlemen of brave mettle; you would lift the moon out of her sphere, if she would continue in it five weeks without changing.

Enter ARIEL, *invisible, playing solemn music.*

SEBASTIAN

We would so, and then go a bat-fowling.

181–2 *I will not . . . so weakly*   I will not lower myself that far.

188 *Do not . . . of it*   don't fight against sleep.

ANTONIO

Nay, good my lord, be not angry.   180

GONZALO

No, I warrant you. I will not adventure my
discretion so weakly. Will you laugh me asleep,
for I am very heavy?

ANTONIO

Go sleep, and hear us.

All are now asleep except ALONSO, SEBASTIAN *and* ANTONIO.

ALONSO

What, all so soon asleep! I wish mine eyes   185
Would, with themselves, shut up my thoughts.
   I find
They are inclined to do so.

SEBASTIAN

                    Please you, sir,
Do not omit the heavy offer of it.
It seldom visits sorrow. When it doth,
It is a comforter.

ANTONIO

                    We two, my lord,   190
Will guard your person while you take your rest,
And watch your safety.

ALONSO

                    Thank you. – Wondrous heavy.

He falls asleep

Exit ARIEL

SEBASTIAN

What a strange drowsiness possesses them!

196 **disposed** wanting.

   nimble lively.

197 **as by consent** as if by agreement.

200 **methinks** I think.

201 **Th' occasion speaks thee** the opportunity speaks to you, calls you.

207 **repose** rest, sleep.

ANTONIO

  It is the quality o' the climate.

SEBASTIAN

                    Why

  Doth it not then *our* eyelids sink? I find not   195
  Myself disposed to sleep.

ANTONIO

                 Nor I; my spirits are nimble.
  They fell together all, as by consent;
  They dropped, as by a thunder-stroke. What might,
  Worthy Sebastian . . .? – Oh, what might . . .? –
                   No more –
  And yet methinks I see it in thy face,   200
  What thou shouldst be. Th' occasion speaks
     thee; and
  My strong imagination sees a crown
  Dropping upon thy head.

SEBASTIAN

              What, art thou waking?

ANTONIO

  Do you not hear me speak?

SEBASTIAN

              I do; and surely
  It is a sleepy language, and thou speak'st   205
  Out of thy sleep. What is it thou didst say?
  This is a strange repose, to be asleep
  With eyes wide open; standing, speaking, moving,
  And yet so fast asleep.

ANTONIO

           Noble Sebastian,

210 **wink'st**   keep your eyes closed.

211 **Whiles**   whilst.

213 **my custom**   I usually am.

214–15 **if heed me . . . thee o'er**   if you listen to me it makes you three times greater.

215 **standing water**   moving neither one way or the other.

216–17 **ebb . . . instructs me**   my natural laziness (or perhaps the accident of birth which made me born second) teaches me to turn down the offer of fortune.

218–19 **If you but knew . . . mock it**   if only you realised how you nurture ambition while you mock it in this way.

222 **sloth**   laziness.

say on   explain further.

223 **setting**   stare, fixed look.

224 **A matter**   some important matter.

224–5 **birth, indeed . . . much to yield**   a new idea which it pains you to speak of.

226 **weak remembrance**   poor memory.

Thou let'st thy fortune sleep - die, rather; wink'st 210
Whiles thou art waking.

SEBASTIAN

                  Thou dost snore distinctly;
There 's meaning in thy snores.

ANTONIO

I am more serious than my custom. You
Must be so too, if heed me; which to do
Trebles thee o'er.

SEBASTIAN

                  Well, I am standing water.   215

ANTONIO

I 'll teach you how to flow.

SEBASTIAN

                Do so. To ebb
Hereditary sloth instructs me.

ANTONIO

              Oh,
If you but knew how you the purpose cherish
Whiles thus you mock it! how, in stripping it,
You more invest it! Ebbing men, indeed,   220
Most often do so near the bottom run
By their own fear or sloth.

SEBASTIAN

            Prithee, say on.
The setting of thine eye and cheek proclaim
A matter from thee; and a birth, indeed,
Which throes thee much to yield.

ANTONIO

              Thus, sir: 225
Although this lord of weak remembrance, this,

227 **be of as little memory**   be as little remembered.

228 **earthed**   buried.

229–30 **only Professes to persuade**   only pretends to convince (knowing Ferdinand is dead).

231–2 **'T is as impossible . . . here swims**   these lines show Antonio's absolute belief that Ferdinand is dead.

233–4 **out of that 'no hope' . . . have you!**   because Ferdinand is dead you are closer to the throne, thus hope to be king.

236 **wink**   snatched look (i.e. even ambition cannot look for a higher goal).

241–4 **Ten leagues . . . razorable**   this exaggerated image suggests that Claribel, in Tunis, is too far from Naples to take the throne.

244 **that from whom**   who, as we travelled from.

Who shall be of as little memory
When he is earthed, hath here almost persuaded –
For he 's a spirit of persuasion, only
Professes to persuade – the King his son 's alive,   230
'T is as impossible that he 's undrowned
As he that sleeps here swims.

SEBASTIAN

                   I have no hope
That he 's undrowned.

ANTONIO

            Oh, out of that 'no hope'
What great hope have you! No hope that way is
Another way so high a hope, that even   235
Ambition cannot pierce a wink beyond,
But doubt discovery there. Will you grant with me
That Ferdinand is drowned?

SEBASTIAN

              He 's gone.

ANTONIO

                Then tell me,
Who 's the next heir of Naples?

SEBASTIAN

           Claribel.

ANTONIO

She that is Queen of Tunis; she that dwells   240
Ten leagues beyond man's life; she that from
    Naples
Can have no note, unless the sun were post –
The man i' the moon 's too slow – till new-born
    chins
Be rough and razorable; she that from whom

245 *cast again*   thrown back on shore.

247–8 *what's past . . . my discharge*   everything that's happened so far was merely leading up to what will happen. The suggestion is that this was all part of fate's plan.

250 *'twixt*   between.

251 *space*   distance.

cubit   an ancient measure: 18 to 22 inches.

253 *Measure*   transport.

254 *wake*   i.e. wake up to this opportunity.

this   i.e. their present sleep.

256 *There be that*   there are others who.

257 *prate*   chatter, gabble.

258 *amply*   fully.

259–60 *I myself . . . deep chat*   I could teach a jackdaw to speak as sensibly as him.

260 *bore*   had.

261–2 *What a sleep . . . advancement*   how opportune this sleep is for you to rise in greatness.

263–4 *does your content . . . fortune*   what do you think of your good fortune?

265 *supplant*   overthrow.

We all were sea-swallowed, though some cast again,   245
And that by destiny, to perform an act
Whereof what 's past is prologue; what to come,
In yours and my discharge.

SEBASTIAN

               What stuff is this? How say you?
'T is true, my brother's daughter's Queen of Tunis;
So is she heir of Naples; 'twixt which regions   250
There is some space.

ANTONIO

             A space whose every cubit
Seems to cry out, 'How shall that Claribel
Measure us back to Naples? Keep in Tunis,
And let Sebastian wake.' Say this were death
That now hath seized them; why, they were no
    worse   255
Than now they are. There be that can rule
    Naples
As well as he that sleeps; lords that can prate
As amply and unnecessarily
As this Gonzalo; I myself could make
A chough of as deep chat. Oh, that you bore   260
The mind that I do! What a sleep were this
For your advancement! Do you understand me?

SEBASTIAN
  Methinks I do.

ANTONIO

          And how does your content
Tender your own good fortune?

SEBASTIAN

              I remember
You did supplant your brother Prospero.

266 **And look how ... upon me**   see how well suited I am to the position (of ruler).

267 **feater**   better.

268 **men**   servants.

270–2 **If 't were ... bosom**   Antonio is not troubled by his conscience, and if it were troubling him like a sore on the foot, he would simply wear slippers.

272–4 **Twenty consciences ... molest**   all the consciences that stand between me and greatness are sugared, or melt like ice, before they cause me pain.

276 **which now he's like, that's dead**   in sleep he has the same appearance as a dead person.

277 **this obedient steel**   his sword, which does what he wants.

278 **lay to bed for ever**   kill.

279 **To the perpetual wink for aye**   endless sleep, death.

280 **This ancient ... Prudence**   he mocks Gonzalo's age and wisdom.

281 **upbraid our course**   say our action is wrong.

282 **take suggestion**   be led by us.

283–4 **They'll tell ... the hour**   the phrase implies that even if we ask them to do something ridiculous, they will do it.

284–5 **Thy case ... precedent**   I will follow your lead (i.e. in taking the dukedom from Prospero).

287 **from the tribute which thou payest**   the duty you must do to the king.

288 **Draw**   we'll take out our swords.

ANTONIO

                                 True: 265
And look how well my garments sit upon me –
Much feater than before. My brother's servants
Were then my fellows; now they are my men.

SEBASTIAN

But for your conscience?

ANTONIO

Ay, sir; where lies that? If 't were a kibe,   270
'T would put me to my slipper. But I feel not
This deity in my bosom. Twenty consciences,
That stand 'twixt me and Milan, candied be they,
And melt, ere they molest! Here lies your brother –
No better than the earth he lies upon,   275
If he were that which now he 's like, that 's
    dead –
Whom I, with this obedient steel, three inches of it,
Can lay to bed for ever; whiles you, doing thus,
To the perpetual wink for aye might put
This ancient morsel, this Sir Prudence, who   280
Should not upbraid our course. For all the rest,
They 'll take suggestion as a cat laps milk;
They 'll tell the clock to any business that
We say befits the hour.

SEBASTIAN

                       Thy case, dear friend,
Shall be my precedent; as thou got'st Milan,   285
I 'll come by Naples. Draw thy sword; one stroke
Shall free thee from the tribute which thou payest;
And I the King shall love thee.

ANTONIO

                      Draw together;

291 **Art** magic.

293 **For else his project dies** otherwise his plan will fail.

300 **sudden** quick.

301 **Preserve** save.

302 **Why are you drawn** why do you have your swords drawn?

304 **securing your repose** keeping you safe in sleep (there may also be a double meaning 'ensuring your rest' by killing you).

And when I rear my hand, do you the like,
To fall it on Gonzalo.

SEBASTIAN

        Oh, but one word. *(He whispers to* ANTONIO*)* 290

Enter ARIEL, *invisible, with music and song.*

ARIEL

My master through his Art foresees the danger
That you, his friend, are in; and sends me forth –
For else his project dies - to keep them living.
        (Sings in GONZALO'S *ear)*

While you here do snoring lie,
Open-eyed Conspiracy   295
   His time doth take.
If of life you keep a care,
Shake off slumber, and beware.
   Awake, Awake!

ANTONIO

Then let us both be sudden.

GONZALO

        (Waking) Now, good angels   300
Preserve the King! *(The others wake up.)*

ALONSO

Why, how now? Ho, awake? *(To* SEBASTIAN *and*
        ANTONIO*)* Why are you drawn?
Wherefore this ghastly looking? What 's the
   matter?

SEBASTIAN

Whiles we stood here securing your repose,
Even now, we heard a hollow burst of bellowing   305

308 *fright* frighten.

315 *verily* true.

316 *quit* leave.

Like bulls, or rather lions. Did 't not wake you?
It struck mine ear most terribly.

ALONSO

I heard nothing.

ANTONIO

Oh, 't was a din to fright a monster's ear,
To make an earthquake! Sure, it was the roar
Of a whole herd of lions.

ALONSO

Heard you this, Gonzalo?   310

GONZALO

Upon mine honour, sir, I heard a humming,
And that a strange one too, which did awake me.
I shaked you, sir, and cried. As mine eyes opened,
I saw their weapons drawn. There was a noise,
That 's verily. 'T is best we stand upon our guard, 315
Or that we quit this place; let 's draw our
    weapons.

ALONSO

Lead off this ground; and let 's make further
    search
For my poor son.

GONZALO

Heavens keep him from these beasts!
For he is, sure, i' the island.

ALONSO

Lead away.

ARIEL

(Aside) Prospero my lord shall know what I have
    done.   320

2 **Prosper**   Prospero.

3 **inch-meal**   slow degrees.

4 **needs must**   have to.

4–7 **But they 'll . . . bid 'em**   this implies that these are all things Prospero has made the spirits do in the past.

5 **urchin-shows**   goblins or hedgehogs.

6 **firebrand**   piece of burning wood.

9 **mow**   make faces.

11 **in my barefoot way**   in my path, where I walk barefooted.

13 **cloven**   split.

17 **Perchance**   perhaps.

   mind   notice.

18 **bear off**   shelter from.

20 **Yond**   over there, that.

So, King, go safely on to seek thy son.

Exeunt

Scene two

Another part of the island.

Enter CALIBAN *with a load of wood. A noise of thunder.*

CALIBAN

All the infections that the sun sucks up
From bogs, fens, flats, on Prosper fall, and make him
By inch-meal a disease! His spirits hear me,
And yet I needs must curse. But they 'll nor pinch,
Fright me with urchin-shows, pitch me i' the mire,   5
Nor lead me, like a firebrand, in the dark
Out of my way, unless he bid 'em. But
For every trifle are they set upon me;
Sometime like apes, that mow and chatter at me,
And after bite me; then like hedgehogs, which   10
Lie tumbling in my barefoot way, and mount
Their pricks at my footfall; sometime am I
All wound with adders, who with cloven tongues
Do hiss me into madness.

Enter TRINCULO.

Lo, now, lo!
Here comes a spirit of his, and to torment me   15
For bringing wood in slowly. I 'll fall flat;
Perchance he will not mind me.

TRINCULO

Here 's neither bush nor shrub, to bear off any
weather at all, and another storm brewing. I hear
it sing i' the wind. Yond same black cloud, yond   20

21 **bombard**   leather container for alcohol.

22 **liquor**   the contents, perhaps alcohol.

24 **cannot choose . . . pailfuls**   will be bound to rain heavily.

27–8 **not of the newest Poor-John**   a large salted hake that is going off.

28–31 **Were I . . . monster make a man**   Trinculo says that so strange is this
       creature (Caliban under the gaberdine) that even a painting of him at a
       fairground would bring in so much money from people wanting to see
       him, that someone would make a fortune.

34 **a dead Indian**   Indians were brought to England as a curiosity, but they
       often died.

   Legged   with legs.

40 **gaberdine**   loose outer clothing.

   hereabout   nearby.

41 **Misery acquaints . . . bedfellows**   in desperate situations it is surprising with
       whom one will sleep (or team up).

42 **shroud**   shelter.

   dregs   last.

46–7 **at a man's funeral**   at a time when people have died; perhaps he even
       refers to Trinculo.

48 **master**   captain.

   swabber   crew member who cleans (swabs) the decks.

huge one, looks like a foul bombard that would
shed his liquor. If it should thunder as it did
before, I know not where to hide my head; yond
same cloud cannot choose but fall by pailfuls.
What have we here? A man or a fish? Dead or   25
alive? A fish. He smells like a fish; a very ancient
and fish-like smell; a kind of, not of the newest
Poor-John. A strange fish! Were I in England now,
as once I was, and had but this fish painted, not a
holiday fool there but would give a piece of silver;   30
there would this monster make a man. Any strange
beast there makes a man. When they will not give
a doit to relieve a lame beggar, they will lay out ten
to see a dead Indian. Legged like a man! And his
fins like arms! Warm o' my troth! I do now let   35
loose my opinion, hold it no longer: this is no
fish, but an islander, that hath lately suffered by
a thunderbolt. *(Thunder again.)* Alas, the storm is
come again! My best way is to creep under his
gaberdine; there is no other shelter hereabout.   40
Misery acquaints a man with strange bedfellows.
I will here shroud till the dregs of the storm be
past.

Enter STEPHANO, *carrying a bottle and singing.*

STEPHANO

I shall no more to sea, to sea,
Here shall I die ashore –   45
This is a very scurvy tune to sing at a man's
funeral; well, here 's my comfort. *(Drinks)*

(He sings.)

The master, the swabber, the boatswain, and I,
The gunner, and his mate,

52 *tang*   sting.

54 *savour*   smell.

55 *scratch . . . did itch*   satisfy her sexual needs.

57 *scurvy*   vile.

58 *Do not torment me – Oh*   Caliban believes this is the beginning of his torture from Prospero using spirits.

60 *Ind*   India.

63 *proper*   fine.

65 *at'*   through his.

68 *an ague*   a fever.

69 *learn*   have learnt.

70–1 *recover him*   make him well.

73 *neat's-leather*   cow-hide or fine leather.

Loved Mall, Meg, and Marian, and Margery,   50
   But none of us cared for Kate.
   For she had a tongue with a tang,
   Would cry to a sailor, Go hang!
She loved not the savour of tar nor of pitch;
Yet a tailor might scratch her where'er she did itch.   55
   Then to sea, boys, and let her go hang!
This is a scurvy tune too. But here 's my comfort.
(Drinks)

CALIBAN

Do not torment me – Oh!

STEPHANO

What 's the matter? Have we devils here? Do you
put tricks upon 's with savages and men of Ind,   60
ha? I have not scaped drowning to be afeared
now of your four legs; for it hath been said, As
proper a man as ever went on four legs cannot
make him give ground; and it shall be said so
 again, while Stephano breathes at' nostrils.   65

CALIBAN

The spirit torments me – Oh!

STEPHANO

This is some monster of the isle with four legs,
who hath got, as I take it, an ague. Where the devil
should he learn our language? I will give him
some relief, if it be but for that. If I can recover   70
him, and keep him tame, and get to Naples with
him, he 's a present for any emperor that ever
trod on neat's-leather.

CALIBAN

Do not torment me, prithee; I 'll bring my wood
home faster.   75

76 **in his fit now**   speaking deleriously in his fever.

76–7 **after the wisest**   sensibly.

80 **I will not take . . . for him**   I won't overprice him (he clearly plans to tame Caliban and sell him as a fairground curiosity).

83 **trembling**   it is presumably Trinculo who is trembling with fright under the gaberdine.

    Prosper   Prospero.

85 **Come on your ways**   come along.

85–6 **Here is that . . . cat**   this refers to the proverb 'ale can make a cat speak'. Stephano clearly thinks this is an animal.

87 **shake**   shake off, end.

89 **chaps**   lips.

93 **forward voice**   voice from the front of his body (i.e. Stephano).

94 **backward voice**   voice at the back of his body (i.e. Caliban).

95 **detract**   take things away.

97 **Amen**   enough.

STEPHANO

He 's in his fit now, and does not talk after the
wisest. He shall taste of my bottle. If he have
never drunk wine afore, it will go near to remove
his fit. If I can recover him, and keep him tame,
I will not take too much for him; he shall pay for   80
him that hath him and that soundly.

CALIBAN

Thou dost me yet but little hurt; thou wilt anon, I
know it by thy trembling. Now Prosper works upon
thee.

STEPHANO

Come on your ways. Open your mouth. Here is   85
that which will give language to you, cat. Open
your mouth; this will shake your shaking, I can
tell you, and that soundly. You cannot tell who 's
your friend. Open your chaps again.

TRINCULO

I should know that voice. It should be – but he is   90
drowned; and these are devils – Oh defend me!

STEPHANO

Four legs and two voices – a most delicate
monster! His forward voice, now, is to speak well
of his friend; his backward voice is to utter foul
speeches and to detract. If all the wine in my   95
bottle will recover him, I will help his ague. Come.
Amen! I will pour some in thy other mouth.

TRINCULO

Stephano!

STEPHANO

Doth thy other mouth call me? Mercy, mercy!

100–1 **I have no long spoon**   from the proverb 'he who sups with the devil must have a long spoon' which advises against forming an alliance with the devil.

102 **thou beest**   you are.

109 **the siege . . . moon-calf**   the excrement of this moon-made creature.

vent   emit, produce as excrement.

115 **scaped**   escaped drowning.

116–7 **Prithee, do not . . . constant**   presumably Trinculo is dancing round with Stephano, or turning him round to inspect him, and Stephano, because he is drunk, is feeling sick.

119 **bears**   carries.

celestial   heavenly.

121 **hither**   here.

123 **butt of sack**   wine sack.

This is a devil, and no monster. I will leave him; I 100
have no long spoon.

TRINCULO

Stephano! If thou beest Stephano, touch me, and
speak to me; for I am Trinculo – be not afeared –
thy good friend Trinculo.

STEPHANO

If thou beest Trinculo, come forth. I 'll pull thee 105
by the lesser legs. If any be Trinculo's legs, these
are they. (*He pulls* TRINCULO *out.*) Thou art very
Trinculo indeed! How cam'st thou to be the
siege of this moon-calf? Can he vent Trinculos?

TRINCULO

I took him to be killed with a thunder-stroke. But 110
art thou not drowned, Stephano? I hope, now,
thou art not drowned. Is the storm over-blown?
I hid me under the dead moon-calf's gaberdine
for fear of the storm. And art thou living,
Stephano? O Stephano, two Neapolitans scaped! 115

STEPHANO

Prithee, do not turn me about; my stomach is not
constant.

CALIBAN

(Aside) These be fine things, an if they be not
sprites. That 's a brave god, and bears celestial
liquor. I will kneel to him.   120

STEPHANO

How didst thou scape? How cam'st thou hither?
Swear, by this bottle, how thou cam'st hither. I
escaped upon a butt of sack, which the sailors
heaved o'erboard, by this bottle! which I made of

128 **the liquor is not earthly**   Caliban has not drunk alcohol before and assumes it is from heaven, hence his reference (which the audience would find comic) to Stephano and Trinculo and gods (lines 119–120).

132 **kiss the book**   the wine bottle has become like a Bible on which to swear.

133 **made like a goose**   the meaning is unclear, perhaps with a swollen groin from venereal disease.

137 **How does thine ague**   how is your fever?

140 **when time was**   once upon a time.

142–3 **and thy dog, and thy bush**   symbols of the man in the moon.

the bark of a tree with mine own hands, since I was 125
cast ashore.

CALIBAN

I 'll swear, upon that bottle, to be thy true subject;
for the liquor is not earthly.

STEPHANO

Here; swear, then, how thou escapedst.

TRINCULO

Swum ashore, man, like a duck. I can swim like a 130
duck, I 'll be sworn.

STEPHANO

Here, kiss the book. Though thou canst swim
like a duck, thou art made like a goose.

TRINCULO

O Stephano, hast any more of this?

STEPHANO

The whole butt, man. My cellar is in a rock by the 135
sea-side, where my wine is hid. How now, moon-
calf! How does thine ague?

CALIBAN

Hast thou not dropped from heaven?

STEPHANO

Out o' the moon, I do assure thee. I was the man
i' the moon when time was.   140

CALIBAN

I have seen thee in her, and I do adore thee. My
mistress showed me thee, and thy dog, and thy
bush.

144 *furnish*   fill.

146 *shallow*   superficial.

148 *credulous*   gullible, easily fooled.

149 *sooth*   truth.

152 *perfidious*   disloyal.

153 *rob*   steal.

157 *puppy-headed*   foolish.

161 *in drink*   drunk.

STEPHANO

    Come, swear to that; kiss the book. I will furnish
    it anon with new contents. Swear.   145

TRINCULO

    By this good light, this is a very shallow monster. I
    afeared of him? A very weak monster! The man
    i' the moon! A most poor credulous monster!
    Well drawn, monster, in good sooth!

CALIBAN

    I 'll show thee every fertile inch o' the island; and 150
    I will kiss thy foot. I prithee, be my god.

TRINCULO

    By this light, a most perfidious and drunken
    monster! When 's god 's asleep, he 'll rob his
    bottle.

CALIBAN

    I 'll kiss thy foot; I 'll swear myself thy subject.   155

STEPHANO

    Come on, then; down, and swear.

TRINCULO

    I shall laugh myself to death at this puppy-headed
    monster. A most scurvy monster! I could find in
    my heart to beat him –

STEPHANO

    Come, kiss.   160

TRINCULO

    But that the poor monster 's in drink. An
    abominable monster!

165 **the tyrant**   the evil master (i.e. Prospero).

170 **crabs**   crab apples.

171 **pig-nuts**   ground-nuts.

172 **instruct thee**   teach you.

173 **snare the nimble marmoset**   catch the agile marmoset monkey.

174 **filberts**   hazlenuts.

175 **scamels**   probably seagulls.

183 **No more dams**   this is clearly a method of catching fish.

CALIBAN

  I 'll show thee the best springs; I 'll pluck thee
    berries;
  I 'll fish for thee, and get thee wood enough.
  A plague upon the tyrant that I serve!   165
  I 'll bear him no more sticks, but follow thee,
  Thou wondrous man.

TRINCULO

  A most ridiculous monster, to make a wonder of
  a poor drunkard!

CALIBAN

  I prithee, let me bring thee where crabs grow;   170
  And I with my long nails will dig thee pig-nuts,
  Show thee a jay's nest, and instruct thee how
  To snare the nimble marmoset; I 'll bring thee
  To clustering filberts, and sometimes I 'll get thee
  Young scamels from the rock. Wilt thou go with me? 175

STEPHANO

  I prithee now, lead the way, without any more
  talking. Trinculo, the King and all our company
  else being drowned, we will inherit here. Here,
  bear my bottle. Fellow Trinculo, we 'll fill him by
  and by again.   180

CALIBAN

  (Sings drunkenly) Farewell, master; farewell, farewell!

TRINCULO

  A howling monster; a drunken monster!

CALIBAN

  No more dams I 'll make for fish
    Nor fetch in firing
    At requiring,   185

186 ***scrape trenchering***   cleaning the wood on which meat was cut.

Nor scrape trenchering, nor wash dish.
   'Ban, 'Ban, Cacaliban
Has a new master - get a new man.

Freedom, high-day! high-day, freedom! freedom,
high-day, freedom!   190

STEPHANO
O brave monster! lead the way.

                                        Exuent

Act 3: summary

Ferdinand is dutifully carrying logs when Miranda takes pity on him and offers to help. They promise themselves to one another, and Prospero, who is looking on from a distance, is pleased they have such loyalty to each other – this was what he intended should happen when he planned that they should meet.

Stephano and Trinculo are drinking with Caliban who tells them about his life on the island. Ariel enters and adds comedy by speaking whilst invisible, causing confusion and argument between the three of them. They plot to kill Prospero. Hearing music made by Ariel, Stephano and Trinculo are afraid, but Caliban reassures them that this is just part of the island's noise and not a danger.

On another part of the island the king and his men search for Ferdinand, watched unseen by Prospero and Ariel. Ariel causes spirits to conjure up a meal which they present and then he makes it disappear. Appearing as a harpy Ariel confronts Alonso, Antonio and Sebastian with the evil they have done against Prospero, and tells Alonso that the fates have chosen their punishment in killing Ferdinand, his son.

Prospero congratulates Ariel on his work. Once Prospero and Ariel have gone, the noblemen wonder at what they have seen and Alonso acknowledges that Ferdinand must be dead. Sebastian and Antonio, unmoved by guilt, set off to fight against the monsters of the island. Alonso is entirely repentant and Gonzalo realises that they must all be affected by the guilt of what they have done in the past.

(Opposite) Bob Peck as Caliban: Royal Shakespeare Company, 1982.

1–2 ***There be some . . . sets off***   some pastimes, although painful, do eventually bring greater pleasure.

  2 ***baseness***   humiliation.

  5 ***but***   if it weren't for the fact that.

  6 ***quickens***   brings to life.

  8 ***crabbed***   bad-tempered.

  9 ***composed***   made up.

 11 ***Upon a sore injunction***   or will be severely punished.

12–13 ***such baseness . . . executor***   there has never been such a noble execution of humble tasks.

 13 ***I forget***   Ferdinand seems to be pausing in work, forgetting the task because he thinks of Miranda.

 14 ***labours***   work.

 15 ***Most busy . . . I do it***   the meaning is disputed, either, 'I may not be working but my mind is busy' or 'I am busiest when I stop working' (to think of Miranda).

 17 ***enjoined***   bound by oath.

 18 ***this***   i.e. the wood.

Act Three

Scene one

In front of Prospero's cell.

Enter FERDINAND, *carrying a log.*

FERDINAND

There be some sports are painful, and their labour
Delight in them sets off. Some kinds of baseness
Are nobly undergone, and most poor matters
Point to rich ends. This my mean task
Would be as heavy to me as odious, but   5
The mistress which I serve quickens what 's dead,
And makes my labours pleasures. Oh, she is
Ten times more gentle than her father 's crabbed,
And he 's composed of harshness. I must remove
Some thousands of these logs, and pile them up,   10
Upon a sore injunction. My sweet mistress
Weeps when she sees me work, and says, such
     baseness
Had never like executor. I forget.
But these sweet thoughts do even refresh my
     labours,
Most busy least, when I do it.

Enter MIRANDA; *and* PROSPERO *unseen.*

MIRANDA

                    Alas now, pray you   15
Work not so hard. I would the lightning had
Burnt up those logs that you are enjoined to pile!
Pray, set it down, and rest you. When this burns,

127

21 **He 's safe**   he is safely occupied; you are safe from him.

22 **discharge**   finish.

24 **the while**   for a while, while you rest.

26 **crack my sinews**   strain my muscles.

27 **such dishonour undergo**   be dishonoured in that way.

28 **become**   suit.

30 **my good will is to it**   my desire is in it.

31 **worm**   creature.

31–2 **thou art . . . shows it**   Prospero says that Miranda has clearly fallen hopelessly in love, just as one may be infected with the plague, against ones will.

33–4 **'T is fresh . . . at night**   Miranda has the power to revitalise Ferdinand, to make night into day.

34 **beseech**   beg.

35 **Chiefly**   mainly.

   set it   use it.

'T will weep for having wearied you. My father
Is hard at study. Pray, now, rest yourself.   20
He 's safe for these three hours.

FERDINAND

                Oh most dear mistress,
The sun will set before I shall discharge
What I must strive to do.

MIRANDA

              If you 'll sit down,
I 'll bear your logs the while. Pray give me that;
I 'll carry it to the pile.

FERDINAND

              No, precious creature.   25
I had rather crack my sinews, break my back,
Than you should such dishonour undergo,
While I sit lazy by.

MIRANDA

           It would become me
As well as it does you, and I should do it
With much more ease, for my good will is to it,   30
And yours it is against.

PROSPERO

          (Aside) Poor worm, thou art infected!
This visitation shows it.

MIRANDA

          You look wearily.

FERDINAND

No, noble mistress. 'T is fresh morning with me
When you are by at night. I do beseech you –
Chiefly that I might set it in my prayers –   35
What is your name?

37 **hest**   command, orders.

Miranda   Miranda means 'to be admired'.

41–2 **The harmony . . . diligent ear**   I have too easily fallen for what they have said.

44–6 **some defect . . . the foil**   none of the women Ferdinand has previously loved has been faultless, their fault has shown up against their virtue.

50 **glass**   mirror.

51 **More that I may call men**   in this description Caliban is not counted as a man.

52–3 **How features . . . skilless of**   I know nothing of how people look in the world at large.

54 **The jewel in my dower**   the greatest gift of my dowry.

57 **to like of**   that I would like.

prattle   talk, chatter.

58 **precepts**   commands, principles.

59 **in my condition**   in my present position.

MIRANDA

                Miranda. O my father,
I have broke your hest to say so!

FERDINAND

                  Admired Miranda!
Indeed the top of admiration! worth
What 's dearest to the world! Full many a lady
I have eyed with best regard, and many a time   40
The harmony of their tongues hath into bondage
Brought my too diligent ear. For several virtues
Have I liked several women; never any
With so full soul, but some defect in her
Did quarrel with the noblest grace she owed,   45
And put it to the foil. But you, oh you,
So perfect and so peerless, are created
Of every creature's best!

MIRANDA

              I do not know
One of my sex; no woman's face remember,
Save, from my glass, mine own. Nor have I seen   50
More that I may call men than you, good friend,
And my dear father. How features are abroad,
I am skilless of; but, by my modesty,
The jewel in my dower, I would not wish
Any companion in the world but you;   55
Nor can imagination form a shape,
Besides yourself, to like of. But I prattle
Something too wildly, and my father's precepts
I therein do forget.

FERDINAND

            I am, in my condition,
A prince, Miranda; I do think, a king;   60

61 *I would not so!* I wish it were not so; for Ferdinand to be king his father must be dead.

endure put up with.

63 *flesh-fly* a fly that carries germs.

blow lay eggs on.

65 *resides* it lives.

66 *and for your sake* in order to serve you, or win you.

69 *kind event* a fortunate outcome.

70 *hollowly* I am telling lies.

70–1 *invert . . . mischief* turn to ill fortune any good I might have had.

72 *Beyond all limit . . . world* much more than all the world.

75 *rare* unusual and fine.

76 *On that which . . . between 'em* on their love, or perhaps their offspring.

Wherefore why.

77–9 *that dare . . . die to want* Miranda shows she has strong feelings and also appropriate reserve.

80–1 *And all the more . . . it shows* the more I try to cover my feelings the more they show (perhaps also alluding to pregnancy.)

I would not so! – and would no more endure
This wooden slavery than to suffer
The flesh-fly blow my mouth. Hear my soul speak:
The very instant that I saw you, did
My heart fly to your service; there resides,   65
To make me slave to it; and for your sake
Am I this patient log-man.

MIRANDA

          Do you love me?

FERDINAND

O heaven, O earth, bear witness to this sound
And crown what I profess with kind event,
If I speak true! if hollowly, invert   70
What best is boded me to mischief! I,
Beyond all limit of what else i' the world,
Do love, prize, honour you.

MIRANDA

          I am a fool
To weep at what I am glad of.

PROSPERO

          (Aside) Fair encounter
Of two most rare affections! Heavens rain grace   75
On that which breeds between 'em!

FERDINAND

          Wherefore weep you?

MIRANDA

At mine unworthiness, that dare not offer
What I desire to give; and much less take
What I shall die to want. But this is trifling;
And all the more it seeks to hide itself,   80

84 *maid*   unmarried woman, or a virgin who refuses to marry anyone else.

86 *will*   want it.

88–9 *as willing . . . of freedom*   with as much desire as a slave has to be free.

91 *hence*   from now.

thousand thousand   a thousand goodbyes.

92–4 *So glad . . . can be more*   Prospero hints here that he knew this would happen, and perhaps planned it, thus his joy cannot include the wonder and surprise that they feel.

94 *to my book*   his books of magic.

96 *Much business appertaining*   many acts related to this.

The bigger bulk it shows. Hence, bashful cunning!
And prompt me, plain and holy innocence!
I am your wife if you will marry me;
If not, I 'll die your maid. To be your fellow
You may deny me; but I 'll be your servant,   85
Whether you will or no.

FERDINAND

My mistress, dearest.
(He kneels) And I thus humble ever.

MIRANDA

My husband, then?

FERDINAND

Ay, with a heart as willing
As bondage e'er of freedom. Here 's my hand.

MIRANDA

And mine, with my heart in 't. And now farewell   90
Till half an hour hence.

FERDINAND

A thousand thousand!

Exeunt FERDINAND *and* MIRANDA *in different directions*

PROSPERO

So glad of this as they I cannot be,
Who are surprised with all; but my rejoicing
At nothing can be more. I 'll to my book;
For yet, ere supper-time, must I perform   95
Much business appertaining.

Exit

1 **butt is out** container for alcohol is empty.

2–3 **bear up, and board 'em** drink up.

4 **folly** foolishness.

5 **but** only.

6 **brained** of our intelligence.

8 **bid** tell.

9 **almost set** either as the sun, almost gone out (from drinking) or, in a fixed stare.

10 **set** placed.

13 **sack** the wine.

16 **standard** flag carrier.

17 **list** please.

no standard not able to stand unsupported.

Scene two

Another part of the island.

Enter CALIBAN, STEPHANO, *and* TRINCULO.

STEPHANO

Tell not me! When the butt is out, we will drink
water – not a drop before. Therefore bear up, and
board 'em. Servant-monster, drink to me.

TRINCULO

Servant-monster! The folly of this island! They say
there 's but five upon this isle. We are three of   5
them. If the other two be brained like us, the
state totters.

STEPHANO

Drink, servant-monster, when I bid thee. Thy eyes
are almost set in thy head.

TRINCULO

Where should they be set else? He were a brave   10
monster indeed, if they were set in his tail.

STEPHANO

My man-monster hath drowned his tongue in
sack. For my part, the sea cannot drown me; I
swam, ere I could recover the shore, five-and-
thirty leagues off and on. By this light, thou shalt   15
be my lieutenant, monster, or my standard.

TRINCULO

Your lieutenant, if you list; he 's no standard.

STEPHANO

We 'll not run, Monsieur Monster.

19 **go**   walk.

21 **thou beest**   you are.

24 **valiant**   brave, courageous.

25–6 **in case to justle**   in the mood to jostle.

26 **deboshed**   corrupt and over-indulged.

31–2 **such a natural**   so naturally foolish.

35 **a mutineer**   a sailor who rebels against authority.

the next tree!   then you shall be hung from the next tree.

39 **hearken**   listen.

suit   request.

TRINCULO

Nor go neither; but you 'll lie like dogs, and yet say
nothing neither.   20

STEPHANO

Moon-calf, speak once in thy life, if thou beest
a good moon-calf.

CALIBAN

How does thy honour? Let me lick thy shoe. I 'll
not serve *him*; he is not valiant.

TRINCULO

Thou liest, most ignorant monster! I am in case to   25
justle a constable. Why, thou deboshed fish, thou,
was there ever man a coward that hath drunk so
much sack as I today. Wilt thou tell a monstrous lie,
being but half a fish and half a monster?

CALIBAN

Lo, how he mocks me! Wilt thou let him, my lord?   30

TRINCULO

'Lord,' quoth he? That a monster should be such
a natural!

CALIBAN

Lo, lo, again! Bite him to death, I prithee.

STEPHANO

Trinculo, keep a good tongue in your head. If you
prove a mutineer – the next tree! The poor   35
monster 's my subject, and he shall not suffer
indignity.

CALIBAN

I thank my noble lord. Wilt thou be pleased to
hearken once again to the suit I made to thee?

40 *Marry* indeed.

43 *cunning* cleverness.

49 *in 's tale* while he tells his story.

50 *supplant* knock out.

52 *Mum* be quiet.

   Proceed carry on.

54 *got* took.

55 *Revenge it on him* take my revenge on him.

STEPHANO

    Marry, will I. Kneel and repeat it. I will stand, and   40
so shall Trinculo.

Enter ARIEL, *invisible.*

CALIBAN

    As I told thee before, I am subject to a tyrant,
A sorcerer, that by his cunning hath cheated me
Of the island.

ARIEL

    Thou liest.   45

CALIBAN

    'Thou liest,' thou jesting monkey, thou!
I would my valiant master would destroy thee!
I do not lie.

STEPHANO

    Trinculo, if you trouble him any more in 's tale, by
this hand, I will supplant some of your teeth.   50

TRINCULO

    Why, I said nothing.

STEPHANO

    Mum, then, and no more. *(To* CALIBAN*)* Proceed.

CALIBAN

    I say, by sorcery he got this isle;
From me he got it. If thy greatness will
Revenge it on him – for I know thou dar'st,   55
But this thing dare not –

STEPHANO

    That 's most certain.

59 **compassed**   won.

60 **the party**   the person you speak of.

61 **I'll yield . . . asleep**   give him to you when he's asleep.

64 **pied ninny**   multicoloured fool. A jester would have worn clothes of many colours.

 patch   jester, in patched clothes.

67 **nought**   nothing.

68 **quick freshes**   freshwater springs.

69 **run into**   don't risk any.

71–2 **make a stockfish of thee**   beat you until you are tender (as a stockfish is beaten before boiling).

73 **did I**   did I do.

CALIBAN

Thou shalt be lord of it, and I 'll serve thee.

STEPHANO

How now shall this be compassed? Canst thou
bring me to the party?   60

CALIBAN

Yea, yea, my lord. I 'll yield him thee asleep,
Where thou mayst knock a nail into his head.

ARIEL

Thou liest; thou canst not.

CALIBAN

What a pied ninny 's this! *(To* TRINCULO*)* Thou
    scurvy patch!
(To STEPHANO*)* I do beseech thy greatness, give
    him blows   65
And take his bottle from him. When that 's gone,
He shall drink nought but brine, for I 'll not
    show him
Where the quick freshes are.

STEPHANO

Trinculo, run into no further danger. Interrupt
the monster one word further, and, by this hand,   70
I 'll turn my mercy out o' doors, and make a
stockfish of thee.

TRINCULO

Why, what did I? I did nothing. I 'll go farther off.

STEPHANO

Didst thou not say he lied?

ARIEL

Thou liest.   75

76 **As** if.

78 **Out o' your wits** mad.

79–80 **A pox . . . drinking do** damn your drink; this is what happens when you drink.

80 **murrain** plague.

83 **forward** carry on.

84 **farther off** further away.

90 **brain him** dash out his brains.

92 **paunch** stab in the stomach.

93 **wezand** windpipe.

95 **sot** fool.

96 **to command** under his command.

97 **rootedly** deep.

Burn but could mean 'only burn his books' or, 'remember you must burn his books'.

STEPHANO

Do I so? Take thou that. *(He hits* TRINCULO.*)* As you
like this, give me the lie another time.

TRINCULO

I did not give the lie. Out o' your wits, and hearing
too? A pox o' your bottle! This can sack and
drinking do. A murrain on your monster, and the   80
devil take your fingers!

CALIBAN

Ha, ha, ha!

STEPHANO

(To CALIBAN*)* Now, forward with your tale.
(To TRINCULO*)* Prithee, stand farther off.

CALIBAN

Beat him enough. After a little time,   85
I 'll beat him too.

STEPHANO

(To TRINCULO*)* Stand farther. – *(To* CALIBAN*)* Come,
proceed.

CALIBAN

Why, as I told thee, 't is a custom with him
I' th' afternoon to sleep. There thou mayst brain
  him,   90
Having first seized his books; or with a log
Batter his skull, or paunch him with a stake,
Or cut his wezand with thy knife. Remember
First to possess his books; for without them
He 's but a sot, as I am, nor hath not   95
One spirit to command. They all do hate him
As rootedly as I. Burn but his books.

145

99 **deck withal**   use for decoration.

102 **a nonpareil**   one without comparison.

103 **dam**   mother.

104 **surpasseth**   outshines.

105 **brave**   excellent.

106 **Ay**   yes.

   become   befit, grace.

107 **bring thee forth brave brood**   bear an excellent family of children.

110 **viceroys**   governors acting for the king and queen.

111 **plot**   plan.

He has brave utensils – for so he calls them –
Which, when he has a house, he 'll deck withal.
And that most deeply to consider is   100
The beauty of his daughter. He himself
Calls her a nonpareil. I never saw a woman
But only Sycorax my dam and she;
But she as far surpasseth Sycorax
As great'st does least.

STEPHANO

                Is it so brave a lass?   105

CALIBAN

Ay, lord; she will become thy bed, I warrant,
And bring thee forth brave brood.

STEPHANO

Monster, I will kill this man. His daughter and I
will be king and queen – save our graces! – and
Trinculo and thyself shall be viceroys. Dost thou 110
like the plot, Trinculo?

TRINCULO

Excellent.

STEPHANO

Give me thy hand. I am sorry I beat thee; but,
while thou liv'st, keep a good tongue in thy head.

CALIBAN

Within this half hour will he be asleep.   115
Wilt thou destroy him then?

STEPHANO

              Ay, on mine honour.

ARIEL

This will I tell my master.

119 *jocund*   merry, cheerful.

   troll the catch   sing the round (a song in parts.)

120 ***while-ere***   a short while ago.

121 ***do reason, any reason***   do anything you reasonably ask.

123 **Flout 'em and scout 'em**   sneer at them and put them down.

s.d. ***tabor***   small drum.

127 *same*   the same.

128 **the picture**   perhaps a topical reference to a picture of a bodiless man, also meaning invisible.

130 ***in thy likeness***   in your normal form.

131 ***take't as thou list***   do what you please.

135 *afeard*   scared.

CALIBAN

    Thou mak'st me merry; I am full of pleasure.
    Let us be jocund! Will you troll the catch
    You taught me but while-ere?   120

STEPHANO

    At thy request, monster, I will do reason, any reason. –
    Come on, Trinculo, let us sing.
        Flout 'em and scout 'em,
        And scout 'em and flout 'em;
          Thought is free.   125

CALIBAN

    That 's not the tune.

ARIEL *plays the tune on a tabor and pipe.*

STEPHANO

    What is this same?

TRINCULO

    This is the tune of our catch, played by the picture
    of Nobody.

STEPHANO

    If thou beest a man, show thyself in thy likeness. 130
    If thou beest a devil, take 't as thou list.

TRINCULO

    Oh, forgive me my sins!

STEPHANO

    He that dies pays all debts. I defy thee. Mercy
    upon us!

CALIBAN

    Art thou afeard?   135

138 *airs*   tunes.

139 *twangling instruments*   stringed instruments being plucked.

140 *sometime*   sometimes.

146 *brave*   splendid.

149 *by and by*   soon.

150 *after*   afterwards.

153 *this taborer; he lays it on*   the one who plays the drum, he plays well.

STEPHANO

No, monster, not I.

CALIBAN

Be not afeard; the isle is full of noises,
Sounds and sweet airs, that give delight, and hurt
    not.
Sometimes a thousand twangling instruments
Will hum about mine ears; and sometime voices,   140
That, if I then had waked after long sleep,
Will make me sleep again. And then, in dreaming,
The clouds methought would open, and show
    riches
Ready to drop upon me; that, when I waked,
I cried to dream again.   145

STEPHANO

This will prove a brave kingdom to me, where I shall
have my music for nothing.

CALIBAN

When Prospero is destroyed.

STEPHANO

That shall be by and by. I remember the story.

TRINCULO

The sound is going away; let 's follow it, and after 150
do our work.

STEPHANO

Lead, monster; we 'll follow. I would I could see
this taborer; he lays it on.

TRINCULO

Wilt come? I 'll follow, Stephano.

Exeunt

1 **By 'r lakin**   by the Virgin Mary.

3 **forth-rights and meanders**   straight and winding paths.

4 **needs must**   must of necessity.

5 **attached**   taken over.

7–8 **put off ... my flatterer**   no longer let myself believe in hope (i.e. no longer believe that Ferdinand is alive).

10 **frustrate**   futile.

12 **for one repulse**   because of one rebuff.

13 **resolved**   decided.

 advantage   opportunity.

14 **take throughly**   use to the full.

15 **oppressed**   made weary.

Scene three

Another part of the island.

Enter ALONSO, SEBASTIAN, ANTONIO, GONZALO, ADRIAN,
FRANCISCO, *and others.*

GONZALO

By 'r lakin, I can go no further, sir.
My old bones ache. Here 's a maze trod, indeed,
Through forth-rights and meanders! By your
    patience,
I needs must rest me.

ALONSO

                    Old lord, I cannot blame thee,
Who am myself attached with weariness   5
To the dulling of my spirits. Sit down, and rest.
Even here I will put off my hope, and keep it
No longer for my flatterer. He is drowned
Whom thus we stray to find; and the sea mocks
Our frustrate search on land. Well, let him go.   10

ANTONIO

(Aside to SEBASTIAN) I am right glad that he 's so out
    of hope.
Do not, for one repulse, forgo the purpose
That you resolved t' effect.

SEBASTIAN

            (Aside to ANTONIO) The next advantage
Will we take throughly.

ANTONIO

            (Aside to SEBASTIAN) Let it be tonight;
For, now they are oppressed with travel, they   15

16 **vigilance**   watchfulness.

18 **No more**   speak no more of it.

19 **hark**   listen.

20 **kind keepers**   guardian angels.

21 **drollery**   puppet-show, masque.

22 **unicorns**   mythical creature shaped like a horse with a horn in the centre of its forehead.

23 **phoenix**   mythical creature which rejuvenated itself by emerging from a funeral pyre.

25 **what does else want credit**   anything else which is generally not believed.

27 **Though fools . . . condemn 'em**   the unicorn and the phoenix were both told of in traveller's tales which were generally not believed (but after this experience they will believe anything).

Will not, nor cannot, use such vigilance
As when they are fresh.

SEBASTIAN

   (Aside to ANTONIO) I say, tonight. No more.

Solemn and strange music; and PROSPERO *on the top, invisible.*

ALONSO

What harmony is this? My good friends, hark!

GONZALO

Marvellous sweet music!

*Enter several strange Shapes, bringing in a banquet. They
dance around it, saluting with gentle and formal gestures.
Then, inviting the King and the others to eat, they depart.*

ALONSO

Give us kind keepers, heavens! – What were these? 20

SEBASTIAN

A living drollery. Now I will believe
That there are unicorns; that in Arabia
There is one tree, the phoenix' throne, one
  phoenix
At this hour reigning there.

ANTONIO

      I 'll believe both;
And what does else want credit, come to me, 25
And I 'll be sworn 't is true. Travellers ne'er did lie,
Though fools at home condemn 'em.

GONZALO

       If in Naples
I should report this now, would they believe me?

30 **certes**   certainly.

34 **nay**   no.

34–6 **Honest lord . . . than devils**   Prospero, who knows of Antonio and
Sebastian's plans realises the truth of Gonzalo's words.

36 **muse**   marvel at.

38 **want**   lack, do not have.

39 **dumb discourse**   silent conversation.

Praise in departing   wait until you see how it ends, then you may praise if
you wish.

41 **viands**   food.

If I should say, I saw such islanders? –
For, certes, these are people of the island,   30
Who, though they are of monstrous shape, yet note,
Their manners are more gentle, kind, than of
Our human generation you shall find
Many, nay, almost any.

PROSPERO

(Aside) Honest lord,
Thou hast said well; for some of you there present   35
Are worse than devils.

ALONSO

I cannot too much muse
Such shapes, such gesture, and such sound,
   expressing –
Although they want the use of tongue – a kind
Of excellent dumb discourse.

PROSPERO

(Aside) Praise in departing.

FRANCISCO
They vanished strangely.

SEBASTIAN

No matter, since   40
They have left their viands behind; for we have
   stomachs. –
Will 't please you taste of what is here?

ALONSO

Not I.

GONZALO
Faith, sir, you need not fear. When we were boys,
Who would believe that there were mountaineers

45 **Dew-lapped** having flesh hanging from their necks.

46 **Wallets** sagging protuberances.

46–7 **such men . . . their breasts** Sir Walter Raleigh, a well-known traveller, described men who were apparently neckless.

48–9 **Each putter-out . . . warrant of** travellers would sometimes bet money on themselves before going travelling. If they returned they'd claim five times what they'd wagered.

49 **stand to** approach the table.

50–1 **last, no matter . . . is past** as Ferdinand is dead, nothing else matters.

s.d. **harpy** a mythological creature with the body of a woman and the wings and claws of a bird.

quaint device ingenious trick.

54 **hath to instrument** has to control.

55 **surfeited** full.

57 **inhabit** live.

'mongst men of all men.

59 **such-like valour** similar bravery.

60 **Their proper selves** themselves.

62 **tempered** made.

64–5 **diminish . . . dowle** lose one small feather.

66 **like** similarly.

Dew-lapped like bulls, whose throats had hanging
　　at 'em　　　　　　　　　　　　　　　　　　45
Wallets of flesh? or that there were such men
Whose heads stood in their breasts? which now we
　　find
Each putter-out of five for one will bring us
Good warrant of.

ALONSO

　　　　　　　I will stand to, and feed,
Although my last, no matter, since I feel　　　　50
The best is past. Brother, my lord the duke,
Stand to, and do as we.

Thunder and lightning. Enter ARIEL *like a harpy, claps his
wings upon the table; and, with a quaint device, the banquet
vanishes.*

ARIEL

You are three men of sin, whom Destiny –
That hath to instrument this lower world
And what is in 't – the never-surfeited sea　　　55
Hath caused to belch up you; and on this island,
Where man doth not inhabit – you 'mongst men
Being most unfit to live. I have made you mad;
And even with such-like valour men hang and
　　drown
Their proper selves. (ALONSO, SEBASTIAN *and* ANTONIO
draw their swords.) You fools! I and my fellows　60
Are ministers of Fate. The elements,
Of whom your swords are tempered, may as well
Wound the loud winds, or with bemocked-at stabs
Kill the still-closing waters, as diminish
One dowle that 's in my plume. My fellow-ministers　65
Are like invulnerable. If you could hurt,

67 **massy** heavy.

69 **For that's my business to you** for my business is to make you do so.

70 **supplant** oust, uproot.

71 **requit it** repayed the deed.

73 **powers** the gods who have the power over fate.

74 **Incensed** made angry.

76 **bereft** deprived.

77 **perdition** loss, hell.

78–9 **attend . . . ways** be with you as you journey on.

79 **wraths** anger.

80 **desolate** isolated, lost.

81–2 **is nothing . . . life ensuing** only a pure life and deep repentance (can save you from the anger of the gods).

s.d. **mows** grimaces.

83 **Bravely** excellently.

84 **a grace it had devouring** it (the performance) had a ravishing or captivating grace.

85 **bated** left out.

86 **So** in the same way.

87 **observation strange** careful attention.

meaner lesser.

88 **Their several kinds have done** have acted their parts as they should.

high charms higher spells.

89 **all knit up** all caught up.

90 **distraction** distracted thoughts.

91 **these fits** this state of madness.

Your swords are now too massy for your strengths,
And will not be uplifted. But remember –
For that 's my business to you – that you three
From Milan did supplant good Prospero;   70
Exposed unto the sea, which hath requit it,
Him and his innocent child; for which foul deed
The powers, delaying, not forgetting, have
Incensed the seas and shores, yea, all the creatures,
Against your peace. Thee of thy son, Alonso, 75
They have bereft; and do pronounce by me
Ling'ring perdition – worse than any death
Can be at once – shall step by step attend
You and your ways; whose wraths to guard you
 from –
Which here, in this most desolate isle, else falls 80
Upon your heads – is nothing but heart's sorrow
And a clear life ensuing.

He vanishes in thunder; then, to soft music, enter the Shapes
again, and dance, with mocks and mows, and carry out the
table.

PROSPERO
 Bravely the figure of this harpy hast thou
 Performed, my Ariel; a grace it had devouring.
 Of my instruction hast thou nothing bated 85
 In what thou hadst to say. So, with good life
 And observation strange, my meaner ministers
 Their several kinds have done. My high charms
  work,
 And these mine enemies are all knit up
 In their distractions. They now are in my power; 90
 And in these fits I leave them, while I visit
 Young Ferdinand – whom they suppose is
  drowned –

93 *And his and mine loved darling*   i.e. Miranda.

96 *billows*   great waves.

99 *Prosper*   Prospero.

    bass my trespass   tell me of my guilty sin.

100 *Therefor*   which is why.

    i' th' ooze is bedded   sleeps at the bottom of the sea.

101 *e'er plummet sounded*   than has ever been reached.

105 *Like poison . . . after*   like slow acting poison.

106 *'gins*   begins.

    bite the spirits   affect their mood.

107 *That are of suppler joints*   who are younger.

108 *hinder*   hold them back.

    ecstasy   madness.

And his and mine loved darling.

Exit

GONZALO

I' the name of something holy, sir, why stand you
In this strange stare?

ALONSO

                  Oh, it is monstrous, monstrous!   95
Methought the billows spoke, and told me of it;
The winds did sing it to me; and the thunder,
That deep and dreadful organ-pipe, pronounced
The name of Prosper. It did bass my trespass.
Therefor my son i' th' ooze is bedded, and   100
I 'll seek him deeper than e'er plummet sounded,
And with him there lie mudded.

Exit

SEBASTIAN

                  But one fiend at a time,
I 'll fight their legions o'er.

ANTONIO

              I 'll be thy second.

Exeunt SEBASTIAN *and* ANTONIO

GONZALO

All three of them are desperate. Their great guilt
Like poison given to work a great time after,   105
Now 'gins to bite the spirits. I do beseech you,
That are of suppler joints, follow them swiftly,
And hinder them from what this ecstasy
May now provoke them to.

ADRIAN

          (To GONZALO*)* Follow, I pray you.

Exeunt

Juno, Iris and Ceres: Royal Shakespeare Company, 1982.

Act 4: summary

Prospero explains to Ferdinand that he has been testing him, by giving him the painful and humbling duty of carrying logs. He needed to be sure that Ferdinand was honourable in his love for Miranda, and appreciated her value as a potential wife.

Prospero creates a magical scene giving the appearance that Iris, Ceres and Juno have appeared on the island to bless their forthcoming wedding. During the spectacle Prospero remembers the plot of Trinculo, Stephano and Caliban to kill him. He makes the vision end explaining to Ferdinand that it has been nothing but magic. He then sends Miranda and Ferdinand to his cell and calls Ariel who has already led the three servant-conspirators on a pointless journey through the roughest ground of the island and into the lake nearby.

Prospero sends Ariel on another errand, to collect fine-looking clothes from the cell and hang them on a lime tree. This Ariel does, and Caliban, Stephano and Trinculo enter stealthily, intent on their plot to kill Prospero. Seeing the clothes Trinculo and Stephano try them on. Caliban warns them it is a trick but they are distracted in their dressing up to look like kings. Ariel conjures up spirits in the shape of hounds and they chase the three off.

Ariel enjoys the situation he has caused and Prospero declares that soon Ariel will have his freedom, as all Prospero's enemies are now at his mercy.

1 *austerely*   severely.

2 *Your compensation makes amends*   your reward (i.e. Miranda) makes up for it.

3 *a third of mine own life*   three things have been important to Prospero: Milan, his Studies and Miranda. So he is giving up a third of his life by giving Miranda to Ferdinand.

5 *tender*   give.

   vexations   troubles.

8 *ratify*   confirm, make official my promise of.

9 *boast her off*   boast about her.

11 *halt*   stand still.

12 *Against an oracle*   even if I were told differently by an oracle. An oracle was believed to convey the desires and beliefs of the gods.

13 *acquisition*   object which has been acquired (bought or given).

14 *purchased*   won.

15 *break her virgin-knot*   have sexual relations with her.

16 *sanctimonious*   holy.

17 *rite*   rituals.

18 *aspersion*   graces.

19 *To make this contract grow*   to make the marriage flourish, probably meaning to produce children as well as happiness.

Act Four

Scene one

In front of Prospero's cell.

Enter PROSPERO, FERDINAND, *and* MIRANDA.

PROSPERO

    (To FERDINAND) If I have too austerely punished you,
    Your compensation makes amends; for I
    Have given you here a third of mine own life,
    Or that for which I live; who once again
    I tender to thy hand. All thy vexations   5
    Were but my trials of thy love, and thou
    Hast strangely stood the test. Here, afore Heaven,
    I ratify this my rich gift. O Ferdinand,
    Do not smile at me that I boast her off,
    For thou shalt find she will outstrip all praise,   10
    And make it halt behind her.

FERDINAND

                    I do believe it
    Against an oracle.

PROSPERO

    Then, as my gift, and thine own acquisition
    Worthily purchased, take my daughter. But
    If thou dost break her virgin-knot before   15
    All sanctimonious ceremonies may
    With full and holy rite be ministered,
    No sweet aspersion shall the heavens let fall
    To make this contract grow. But barren hate,

20 **disdain** scorn.

    bestrew cover.

23 **Hymen's lamps** Hymen was the Greek god of marriage, often shown carrying a torch.

24 **issue** offspring.

25 **den** night.

27 **worser genius** bad angel.

    can can make.

28–9 **to take away . . . edge of** to spoil.

30–1 **When I shall . . . below** like the traditional bridegroom, Ferdinand says the day of his wedding will seem so long away, as if Phoebus' horses are lame, and the night kept prisoner in hell. Phoebus was the Greek god of the sun seen as a charioteer.

33 **industrious** hardworking.

34 **potent** powerful.

35 **meaner fellows** lesser spirits.

    service task.

37 **such another** another similar.

    rabble band of spirits.

39 **Incite them to quick motion** make them come here quickly.

40–1 **Bestow upon . . . mine Art** shows this young couple another magic trick.

Sour-eyed disdain and discord shall bestrew   20
The union of your bed with weeds so loathly
That you shall hate it both. Therefore take heed,
As Hymen's lamps shall light you.

FERDINAND
                                        As I hope
For quiet days, fair issue, and long life,
With such love as 't is now, the murkiest den,   25
The most oppórtune place, the strong'st suggestion
Our worser genius can, shall never melt
Mine honour into lust, to take away
The edge of that day's celebration
When I shall think, or Phoebus' steeds are
    foundered,   30
Or Night kept chained below.

PROSPERO
                              Fairly spoke.
Sit, then, and talk with her; she is thine own.
(Aside) What, Ariel! my industrious servant, Ariel!

Enter ARIEL.

ARIEL
What would my potent master? Here I am.

PROSPERO
Thou and thy meaner fellows your last service   35
Did worthily perform; and I must use you
In such another trick. Go bring the rabble –
O'er whom I give thee power – here to this place.
Incite them to quick motion; for I must
Bestow upon the eyes of this young couple   40
Some vanity of mine Art. It is my promise,
And they expect it from me.

42　**Presently?**　straight away?

43　**Ay, with a twink**　yes, in the twinkle of an eye.

47　**mop and mow**　mocking and grimacing faces.

50　**conceive**　understand.

51　**Look thou be true**　make sure you are honest, true to your word.

51–2　**Do not give . . . rein**　do not spend too much time idly flirting with Miranda.

52–3　**The strongest oaths . . . blood**　the fire of passion is such that it can reduce oaths to straw, easily burnt up.

53　**Be more abstemious**　deny yourself pleasure.

54　**good night your vow**　farewell to your promise (not to sleep with Miranda before their wedding day).

　　warrant　guarantee.

55　**The white . . . liver**　the liver was seen as the source of passion in the body. Ferdinand's pure love, and the pure love of Miranda, is therefore able to keep passion at bay.

57–8　**Bring . . . a spirit**　bring too many rather than too few spirits.

58　**pertly**　swiftly.

ARIEL

Presently?

PROSPERO

Ay, with a twink.

ARIEL

Before you can say, 'Come' and 'Go',
And breathe twice, and cry, 'So, so',   45
Each one, tripping on his toe,
Will be here with mop and mow.
Do you love me, master? No?

PROSPERO

Dearly, my delicate Ariel. Do not approach
Till thou dost hear me call.

ARIEL

Well, I conceive.   50

Exit

PROSPERO

(*To* FERDINAND) Look thou be true. Do not give
    dalliance
Too much the rein. The strongest oaths are straw
To the fire i' the blood. Be more abstemious,
Or else, good night your vow!

FERDINAND

I warrant you, sir:
The white cold virgin snow upon my heart   55
Abates the ardour of my liver.

PROSPERO

(*To* FERDINAND) Well.
(*To* ARIEL) Now come, my Ariel! Bring a córollary,
Rather than want a spirit. Appear, and pertly!

59 **No tongue! All Eyes!**   don't speak, just look.

s.d. **Iris**   the Greek goddess of the rainbow and the messenger of the gods.

60 **Ceres**   the goddess of fertility and harvest.

leas   arable fields.

61 **vetches**   plants of the sweet pea family.

pease   pea plant.

63 **meads thatched . . . to keep**   meadows covered with fodder for cattle to keep them over the winter.

65 **spongy**   wet, damp.

at thy hest betrims   decorates at your command.

66 **cold nymphs**   pure young women.

broom-groves   wooded areas where broom grows.

67 **dismisséd**   rejected.

68 **Being lass-lorn**   having lost his loved one.

poll-clipt   edged with poles.

69 **sea-marge**   shoreline.

rocky-hard   rocky outcrop, jetty.

70 **air**   breathe in the air.

the queen o' the sky   Juno.

71 **wat'ry arch**   rainbow.

74 **sport**   play, be entertained.

amain   all at once.

76 **ne'er**   never.

78 **saffron**   orange-red.

79 **Diffusest**   pours.

81 **bosky**   wooded.

(To FERDINAND *and* MIRANDA) No tongue! All eyes!
   Be silent. *(Soft music)*

Enter IRIS.

IRIS

Ceres, most bounteous lady, thy rich leas   60
Of wheat, rye, barley, vetches, oats, and pease;
Thy turfy mountains, where live nibbling sheep,
And flat meads thatched with stover, them to keep;
Thy banks with pionéd and twilléd brims,
Which spongy April at thy hest betrims,   65
To make cold nymphs chaste crowns; and thy
    broom-groves,
Whose shadow the dismisséd bachelor loves,
Being lass-lorn; thy poll-clipt vineyard;
And thy sea-marge, sterile and rocky-hard,
Where thou thyself dost air – the queen o' the sky, 70
Whose wat'ry arch and messenger am I,
Bids thee leave these; and with her sovereign grace,
Here, on this grass-plot, in this very place,
To come and sport. Her peacocks fly amain.

JUNO *descends.*

Approach, rich Ceres, her to entertain.   75

Enter CERES.

CERES

Hail, many-coloured messenger, that ne'er
Dost disobey the wife of Jupiter;
Who, with thy saffron wings, upon my flowers
Diffusest honey-drops, refreshing showers;
And with each end of thy blue bow dost crown 80
My bosky acres and my unshrubbed down,

83 *hither*   here.

85–6 *estate On*   give to.

87 *Venus*   Roman goddess of love.

   her son   Cupid, often shown as blind and shooting arrows which make the most unlikely couples fall in love.

89–91 *The means . . . have forsworn*   I have refused to spend time in the scandalous company of Venus and Cupid.

91 *society*   company.

92 *her deity*   i.e. Venus.

93 *Paphos*   the meeting place of the gods.

94 *Dove-drawn*   carried on the wings of doves.

   thought they to   they had intended to.

95 *wanton*   roguish, playful.

   maid   young girl, virgin.

96 *bed-right*   conjugal rights. (The couple have promised not to have sexual relations.)

97 *Till Hymen's torch be lighted*   until the marriage ceremony is performed.

98 *Mars's hot minion*   Venus, the mistress of the god Mars.

99 *waspish-headed*   peevish.

101 *right out*   entirely.

102 *gait*   manner of approaching.

Rich scarf to my proud earth. Why hath thy queen
Summoned me hither, to this short-grassed green?

IRIS

A contract of true love to celebrate;
And some donation freely to estate   85
On the blest lovers.

CERES

     Tell me, heavenly bow,
If Venus or her son, as thou dost know,
Do now attend the queen? Since they did plot
The means that dusky Dis my daughter got,
Her and her blind boy's scandalled company   90
I have forsworn.

IRIS

     Of her society
Be not afraid. I met her deity
Cutting the clouds towards Paphos, and her son
Dove-drawn with her. Here thought they to have
  done
Some wanton charm upon this man and maid,   95
Whose vows are, that no bed-right shall be paid
Till Hymen's torch be lighted. But in vain;
Mars's hot minion is returned again;
Her waspish-headed son has broke his arrows,
Swears he will shoot no more, but play with
  sparrows,   100
And be a boy right out.

CERES

     Highest queen of state,
Great Juno comes; I know her by her gait.

103 **sister**   Juno and Ceres were the daughters of Saturn.

104 **twain**   couple.

105 **issue**   offspring, children.

110 **foison**   abundance.

111 **garners**   storehouses.

113 **burthen**   burden (of fruit).

114–15 **Spring come . . . harvest**   a traditional saying wishing a speedy spring (and thus a short winter).

119 **be bold**   dare.

120 **spirits**   of the spirit world rather than human.

120 **mine Art**   my magic.

121 **confines**   enclosed areas which they cannot normally leave.

enact   act out.

122 **fancies**   fantastical wishes.

123 **wondered**   miraculous, admirable.

JUNO

How does my bounteous sister? Go with me
To bless this twain, that they may prosperous be,
And honoured in their issue.   105

They sing.

JUNO

Honour, riches, marriage-blessing,
Long continuance, and increasing,
Hourly joys be still upon you!
Juno sings her blessings on you.

CERES

Earth's increase, foison plenty,   110
Barns and garners never empty;
Vines with clust'ring bunches growing;
Plants with goodly burthen bowing;
Spring come to you at the farthest
In the very end of harvest!   115
Scarcity and want shall shun you;
Ceres' blessing so is on you.

FERDINAND

This is a most majestic vision, and
Harmonious charmingly. May I be bold
To think these spirits?

PROSPERO

                    Spirits, which by mine Art   120
I have from their confines called to enact
My present fancies.

FERDINAND

                    Let me live here ever;
So rare a wondered father and a wise
Makes this place Paradise.

126 *mute*   silent.

127 *marred*   spoilt.

128 *Naiads*   Greek mythological water nymphs.

   windring   winding.

129 *sedged*   made of sedge-grass.

130 *crisp channels*   wavy waters.

131 *Answer your summons*   come when you are commanded.

132 *temperate*   chaste, virginal.

138 *country footing*   country dancing.

139 *conspiracy*   evil plot.

140 *the beast*   later in the scene Caliban and his accomplices are described as
   young horses and then foolish calves, emphasising their beast-like nature.

   confederates   allies, comrades.

142 *avoid*   go.

JUNO *and* CERES *whisper, and send* IRIS *on an errand.*

PROSPERO

    (To FERDINAND *and* MIRANDA*).* Sweet, now, silence!
Juno and Ceres whisper seriously.   125
There 's something else to do. Hush, and be mute,
Or else our spell is marred.

IRIS

You nymphs, called Naiads, of the windring brooks,
With your sedged crowns and ever-harmless looks,
Leave your crisp channels, and on this green land   130
Answer your summons. Juno does command.
Come, temperate nymphs, and help to celebrate
A contract of true love; be not too late.

Enter NYMPHS.

You sunburned sicklemen, of August weary,
Come hither from the furrow, and be merry.   135
Make holiday; your rye-straw hats put on,
And these fresh nymphs encounter every one
In country footing.

Enter REAPERS. *They join with the* NYMPHS *in a graceful dance,
towards the end of which* PROSPERO *starts suddenly, and
speaks. There is a strange, hollow, and confused noise, and the*
NYMPHS *and* REAPERS *vanish.*

PROSPERO

    (Aside) I had forgot that foul conspiracy
Of the beast Caliban and his confederates   140
Against my life. The minute of their plot
Is almost come. *(To the Spirits)* Well done! avoid;
    no more!

144 **works**   affects.

145 **distempered**   out of sorts.

146 **a moved sort**   an anxious mood.

148 **revels**   dances or displays.

149 **foretold**   previously told you.

151 **baseless fabric**   without base, made of nothing.

154 **inherit**   possesses.

155 **pageant**   play, performance.

156 **rack**   cloud.

 such-stuff   the sort of thing.

157 **As dreams are made on**   that dreams are made of.

158 **rounded**   surrounded, i.e. before birth and after death there is sleep.

 vexed   worried.

160 **infirmity**   illness.

161 **If you be pleased, retire**   please will you go.

162 **repose**   rest.

FERDINAND

    This is strange. Your father 's in some passion
    That works him strongly.

MIRANDA

                   Never till this day
    Saw I him touched with anger, so distempered.   145

PROSPERO

    You do look, my son, in a moved sort,
    As if you were dismayed. Be cheerful, sir.
    Our revels now are ended. These our actors,
    As I foretold you, were all spirits, and
    Are melted into air, into thin air.   150
    And, like the baseless fabric of this vision,
    The cloud-capped towers, the gorgeous palaces,
    The solemn temples, the great globe itself,
    Yea, all which it inherit, shall dissolve,
    And, like this insubstantial pageant faded,   155
    Leave not a rack behind. We are such stuff
    As dreams are made on; and our little life
    Is rounded with a sleep. Sir, I am vexed.
    Bear with my weakness; my old brain is troubled.
    Be not disturbed with my infirmity.   160
    If you be pleased, retire into my cell,
    And there repose. A turn or two I 'll walk,
    To still my beating mind.

FERDINAND *and* MIRANDA

              We wish your peace.

                          Exeunt

164 **cleave** hold fast.

167 **presented Ceres** this could mean Ariel stage-managed the Ceres scene or that he acted the part of the goddess himself.

168 **thought to have** had intended to.

170 **varlets** rascals.

171 **red-hot** red faced.

172 **valour** courage.

smote struck.

174–5 **bending Towards** pursuing.

175 **tabor** drum.

176 **unbacked colts** young horses not yet broken for riding.

177 **Advanced** lifted.

178 **As** as if.

179 **lowing** low noise made by a cow.

180 **Toothed briers** prickly wild roses.

goss gorse.

182 **filthy-mantled** scum-covered.

184 **O'erstunk** smelt worse than.

PROSPERO

Come with a thought. I thank thee. Ariel, come.

Enter ARIEL.

ARIEL

Thy thoughts I cleave to. What 's thy pleasure?

PROSPERO

                                Spirit,   165

We must prepare to meet with Caliban.

ARIEL

Ay, my commander. When I presented Ceres,
I thought to have told thee of it; but I feared
Lest I might anger thee.

PROSPERO

Say again, where didst thou leave these varlets?   170

ARIEL

I told you, sir, they were red-hot with drinking;
So full of valour that they smote the air
For breathing in their faces; beat the ground
For kissing of their feet; yet always bending
Towards their project. Then I beat my tabor;   175
At which, like unbacked colts, they pricked their
    ears,
Advanced their eyelids, lifted up their noses
As they smelt music. So I charmed their ears,
That, calf-like, they my lowing followed, through
Toothed briers, sharp furzes, pricking goss, and
    thorns,   180
Which entered their frail shins. At last I left them
I' the filthy-mantled pool beyond your cell,
There dancing up to the chins, that the foul lake
O'erstunk their feet.

185 *retain*   keep.

186 *trumpery*   rich-looking clothes.

hither   here.

187 *stale*   a decoy.

188–9 *on whose nature . . . stick*   however much one cares for and teaches him he will behave according to his low breeding.

189–90 *my pains Humanely taken*   the trouble I took to treat him humanely.

190 *lost*   wasted.

192 *cankers*   grows evil.

plague   visit a plague or curse upon.

193 *line*   lime tree.

194 *blind mole*   the mole was believed to have very good hearing.

195 *foot fall*   footstep.

197 *played the Jack*   acted in a knavish fashion, made us look foolish.

PROSPERO
>   This was well done, my bird.
> Thy shape invisible retain thou still.   185
> The trumpery in my house, go bring it hither,
> For stale to catch these thieves.

ARIEL
>   I go, I go.

Exit

PROSPERO
> A devil, a born devil, on whose nature
> Nurture can never stick; on whom my pains,
> Humanely taken, all, all lost, quite lost;   190
> And as with age his body uglier grows,
> So his mind cankers. I will plague them all,
> Even to roaring.

Enter ARIEL, *loaded with shiny clothes, etc.*

>   Come, hang them on this line.

Enter CALIBAN, STEPHANO, *and* TRINCULO, *all wet.* PROSPERO
and ARIEL *remain invisible.*

CALIBAN
> Pray you, tread softly, that the blind mole may not
> Hear a foot fall. We now are near his cell.   195

STEPHANO
> Monster, your fairy, which you say is a harmless
> fairy, has done little better than played the Jack
> with us.

TRINCULO
> Monster, I do smell all horse-piss; at which my
> nose is in great indignation.   200

203 **lost**   done for.

206 **Shall hoodwink this mischance**   will make up for this present misfortune.

   softly   quietly.

211 **my wetting**   being soaked through.

213 **o'er ears**   overheard.

214 **labour**   hard work.

219 **aye**   ever.

STEPHANO

So is mine. Do you hear, monster? If I should
take a displeasure against you, look you –

TRINCULO

Thou wert but a lost monster.

CALIBAN

Good my lord, give me thy favour still.
Be patient, for the prize I 'll bring thee to   205
Shall hoodwink this mischance. Therefore
     speak softly.
All 's hushed as midnight yet.

TRINCULO

Ay, but to lose our bottles in the pool –

STEPHANO

There is not only disgrace and dishonour in that,
     monster, but an infinite loss.   210

TRINCULO

That 's more to me than my wetting. Yet this
is your harmless fairy, monster.

STEPHANO

I will fetch off my bottle, though I be o'er ears for
my labour.

CALIBAN

Prithee, my King, be quiet. See'st thou here,   215
This is the mouth o' the cell. No noise, and
     enter.
Do that good mischief which may make this island
Thine own for ever, and I, thy Caliban,
For aye thy foot-licker.

224 **but trash** worthless.

226 **a frippery** a place where second-hand clothes were sold.

227 **Put off** do not take.

230 **dropsy** sickness where excess water accumulates in a part of the body.

231 **dote** be excessively fond.

    luggage useless rubbish.

    Let 't alone leave it.

232 **murther** murder.

235 **Mistress line** Stephano addresses the lime tree.

236 **jerkin** a short jacket.

    line lime tree; also a pun on the line of the equator – it was a practice to shave the heads of sailors when they crossed the equator for the first time.

237 **like** likely.

239 **line and level** accurately.

    an 't like so please.

STEPHANO

Give me thy hand. I do begin to have bloody 220
thoughts.

TRINCULO

O King Stephano! O peer! O worthy Stephano!
Look what wardrobe here is for thee!

CALIBAN

Let it alone, thou fool; it is but trash.

TRINCULO

Oh, ho, monster! we know what belongs to a 225
frippery. O King Stephano!

STEPHANO

Put off that gown, Trinculo; by this hand, I 'll
have that gown.

TRINCULO

Thy grace shall have it.

CALIBAN

The dropsy drown this fool! What do you mean   230
To dote thus on such luggage? Let 't alone,
And do the murther first. If he awake,
From toe to crown he 'll fill our skins with pinches,
Make us strange stuff.

STEPHANO

Be you quiet, monster. Mistress line, is not this my 235
jerkin? Now is the jerkin under the line: now,
jerkin, you are like to lose your hair, and prove a
bald jerkin.

TRINCULO

Do, do! We steal by line and level, an 't like your
grace.   240

241 *jest*   joke.

244 **pass of pate**   witty comment.

245 *lime*   bird-lime, a sticky substance used to snare or steal birds.

247 **lose our time**   waste the best moment.

248 **barnacles**   geese.

255 **Mountain**   the name of the hound, as are 'Silver', 'Fury' and 'Tyrant' mentioned in the following lines.

STEPHANO

I thank thee for that jest; here 's a garment for 't.
Wit shall not go unrewarded while I am king
of this country. 'Steal by line and level' is an excellent
pass of pate; there 's another garment for 't.

TRINCULO

Monster, come, put some lime upon your fingers,   245
and away with the rest.

CALIBAN

I will have none on 't. We shall lose our time,
And all be turned to barnacles, or to apes
With foreheads villainous low.

STEPHANO

Monster, lay-to your fingers; help to bear this 250
away where my hogshead of wine is, or I 'll turn
you out of my kingdom. Go to, carry this.

TRINCULO

And this.

STEPHANO

Ay, and this.

A noise of hunters heard. Enter several kinds of SPIRITS, *in the
shape of dogs and hounds, hunting them up and down;*
PROSPERO *and* ARIEL *urging them on.*

PROSPERO

Hey, Mountain, hey!   255

ARIEL

Silver! there it goes, Silver!

PROSPER

Fury, Fury! there. Tyrant, there! Hark, hark!

259 **dry convulsions**   tremors believed to be caused by lack of fluid around the joints.

sinews   muscles.

260 **aged**   old people's.

pinch-spotted   blotched with bruises.

261 **pard or cat o' mountain**   leopard.

264 **labours**   efforts.

266 **do me service**   serve me.

CALIBAN, STEPHANO *and* TRINCULO *are driven out.*

Go charge my goblins that they grind their joints
With dry convulsions; shorten up their sinews
With aged cramps; and more pinch-spotted make
    them   260
Than pard or cat o' mountain.

ARIEL

           Hark, they roar!

PROSPERO

Let them be hunted soundly. At this hour
Lies at my mercy all mine enemies.
Shortly shall all my labours end, and thou
Shalt have the air at freedom. For a little   265
Follow, and do me service.

                                Exeunt

Derek Jacobi as Prospero: Royal Shakespeare Company, 1982.

Act 5: summary

Ariel tells Prospero that the king and his followers are 'full of sorrow and weeping' and Prospero decides that he must be merciful. He orders Ariel to bring them to him. He then calls on all the spirits of the island and acknowledges the magic he has used, stating that soon he will give it up and in doing so, symbolically break his staff and throw his book of magic into the sea.

Ariel re-enters with the king and his followers, drawn in by solemn music. Seeing his enemies Prospero speaks about them while they cannot see or hear him. He also speaks about Gonzalo and his goodness.

Prospero sends Ariel to his cell to collect the clothes he wore as Duke of Milan, and also asks him to fetch the sailors left in the ship. Gonzalo recognises Prospero. Prospero introduces himself to Alonso as 'the wronged Duke of Milan' and welcomes him to the island. Alonso is unsure if this is reality or illusion but is convinced as Prospero forgives each one.

Prospero says he lost his daughter in the storm just as Alonso lost his son, and then shows them Miranda and Ferdinand playing chess. There is much celebration and the promise of a royal wedding when they return to Naples. The boatswain enters saying that the ship is as it was, and ready to sail, no longer shipwrecked.

Stephano, Trinculo and Caliban enter. They are drunk and wearing the fine clothes they have stolen. Prospero tells Alonso of their plotting and then sends them off to earn forgiveness. Prospero invites all the noblemen to stay the night in his cell where he will explain everything. He then frees Ariel.

In the Epilogue, Prospero addresses the audience explaining that just as he, as Prospero, has been freed to go back to Milan so he, the actor, now wishes to be free to leave them. He asks for the audience to applaud, thus releasing him.

2 **crack not**   do not explode before their time.

2–3 **and time . . . carriage**   the remaining time is so free from work that it walks upright (without a burden).

3 **How's the day**   what time is it?

7 **How fares**   how is.

   and 's   and his.

8 **gave in charge**   ordered.

10 **line**   lime.

   weather-fends   offers shelter from the weather for.

11 **your release**   you release them.

14 **Brimful**   filled.

15 **termed**   called.

16–17 **winter's drops . . . reeds**   drops of rain or melted snow from the eaves of a thatched roof.

17 **charm**   spell.

Act Five

Scene one

In front of Prospero's cell.

Enter PROSPERO *in his magic robes, and* ARIEL.

PROSPERO

Now does my project gather to a head.
My charms crack not, my spirits obey; and time
Goes upright with his carriage. How 's the day?

ARIEL

On the sixth hour; at which time, my lord,
You said our work should cease.

PROSPERO

                    I did say so,   5
When first I raised the tempest. Say, my spirit,
How fares the King and 's followers?

ARIEL

                  Confined together
In the same fashion as you gave in charge,
Just as you left them; all prisoners, sir,
In the line-grove which weather-fends your cell.   10
They cannot budge till your release. The King,
His brother, and yours, abide all three distracted,
And the remainder mourning over them,
Brimful of sorrow and dismay; but chiefly
Him you termed, sir, 'The good old lord, Gonzalo'.   15
His tears run down his beard, like winter's drops
From eaves of reeds. Your charm so strongly works
   'em,

18   *beheld*   saw.

21   *Hast thou, which are but*   have you, who are only.

23   *kind*   i.e. human.

23–4   *relish . . . as they*   experiencing emotions as sharply as they do.

24   *kindlier*   more fully, with greater sympathy.

25   *high wrongs*   evil deeds.

26–7   *Yet with . . . take part*   I am led by my nobility rather than my anger.

28   *vengeance*   a desire for revenge.

28–30   *They being . . . further*   all I wanted was their repentence and having that I have not got any more cause for anger.

31   *charms*   spells.

32   *themselves*   back to their normal selves.

33   *Ye*   you.

      standing   still.

35   *ebbing Neptune*   sea as it goes out. Neptune was the god of the sea.

      fly him   fly from him.

36   *demi-puppets*   fairies of puppet-like size.

37   *green sour ringlets*   fairy rings.

38   *not bites*   does not bite.

That if you now beheld them, your affections
Would become tender.

PROSPERO

                  Dost thou think so, spirit?

ARIEL

Mine would, sir, were I human.

PROSPERO

                  And mine shall.   20
Hast thou, which art but air, a touch, a feeling
Of their afflictions, and shall not myself,
One of their kind, that relish all as sharply
Passion as they, be kindlier moved than thou art?
Though with their high wrongs I am struck to the
    quick,   25
Yet with my nobler reason 'gainst my fury
Do I take part. The rarer action is
In virtue than in vengeance. They being penitent,
The sole drift of my purpose doth extend
Not a frown further. Go release them, Ariel.   30
My charms I 'll break, their senses I 'll restore,
And they shall be themselves.

ARIEL

                  I 'll fetch them, sir.

                                  Exit

PROSPERO

Ye elves of hills, brooks, standing lakes, and groves;
And ye that on the sands with printless foot
Do chase the ebbing Neptune, and do fly him   35
When he comes back; you demi-puppets that
By moonshine do the green sour ringlets make,
Whereof the ewe not bites; and you whose pastime

39 **to make midnight mushrooms**   as mushrooms appear overnight they were believed to be made by elves.

40 **by whose aid**   with whose help.

41 **bedimmed**   dimmed.

43 **azured vault**   skies.

44 **Set roaring war**   thus he created the tempest.

45 **rifted Jove's stout oak**   split the oak tree (which was sacred to the god Jove).

46 **his own bolt**   Jove was believed to rain down thunderbolts.

47 **spurs**   roots.

49 **oped**   opened up.

50 **potent Art**   strong magic.

   rough magic   unsubtle (because it is to do with controlling objects and weather rather than people's minds).

51 **abdure**   renounce, give up.

   required   sought, requested.

53 **work mine end**   complete my plan.

   their senses, that   those whom.

54 **airy charm**   musical magic.

   staff   the symbol of his magic, like a wand.

56 **than did ever plummet sound**   than sound ever reached.

57 **book**   book of magic.

58 **air**   music.

58–60 **the best . . . thy skull**   music was seen as therapeutic, being able to give comfort to the sick or mentally ill. Here the lords are out of their senses.

61 **spell-stopped**   prevented from moving by the spell upon you.

63–4 **Mine eyes . . .**   just seeing you moves me to pity/sympathy.

64 **fellowly**   sympathetic.

   apace   quickly.

Is to make midnight mushrooms, that rejoice
To hear the solemn curfew; by whose aid   40
(Weak masters though ye be) I have bedimmed
The noontide sun, called forth the mutinous winds,
And 'twixt the green sea and the azured vault
Set roaring war. To the dread rattling thunder
Have I given fire, and rifted Jove's stout oak   45
With his own bolt. The strong-based promontory
Have I made shake, and by the spurs plucked up
The pine and cedar. Graves at my command
Have waked their sleepers, oped, and let 'em forth
By my so potent Art. But this rough magic   50
I here abjure, and, when I have required
Some heavenly music (which even now I do)
To work mine end upon their senses, that
This airy charm is for, I 'll break my staff,
Bury it certain fathoms in the earth,   55
And deeper than did ever plummet sound
I 'll drown my book.

Solemn music

Enter ARIEL. *He is followed by* ALONSO, *frantic, attended by*
GONZALO. SEBASTIAN *and* ANTONIO *follow, also frantic,*
attended by ADRIAN *and* FRANCISCO. *They all enter the circle*
which PROSPERO *has made, and there stand charmed.* PROSPERO
watches them, and then speaks.

A solemn air, and the best comforter
To an unsettled fancy, cure thy brains,
Now useless, boiled within thy skull! There stand,   60
For you are spell-stopped.
Holy Gonzalo, honourable man,
Mine eyes, ev'n sociable to the show of thine,
Fall fellowly drops. The charm dissolves apace;

66–8 **so their . . . clearer reason**   as their senses are reawakened they begin to think more clearly.

69 **preserver**   rescuer, the one who saved my life.

70 **him thou follow'st**   i.e. Prospero.

70–1 **I will pay . . . and deed**   repay you fully in words and actions for the way you treated me.

73 **a furtherer in the act**   one who advanced or forwarded the deed.

74 **pinched**   punished (both literally and by guilt).

75 **entertained**   was led by, pampered by.

76 **remorse and nature**   pity and natural behaviour (both as a human and a nobleman).

77 **inward pinches**   guilty conscience.

79 **Unnatural**   behaving against the natural order of the world. As kings were believed to be chosen by God, to kill a king was a devilish act.

80 **Begins to swell**   increases.

80–2 **and the approaching . . . muddy**   the growing awareness of reason is described as like the gradual rising of the tide on the seashore.

82 **Not one . . . know me**   none can see me and if they could they wouldn't recognise me.

84 **rapier**   sword.

85 **discase**   remove my outer garment.

86 **As I was sometime Milan**   as I looked when I was the duke of Milan.

87 **ere**   before.

90 **couch**   sleep.

And as the morning steals upon the night,　　　　65
Melting the darkness, so their rising senses
Begin to chase the ignorant fumes that mantle
Their clearer reason. O good Gonzalo,
My true preserver, and a loyal sir
To him thou follow'st! I will pay thy graces　　　70
Home both in word and deed. Most cruelly
Didst thou, Alonso, use me and my daughter.
Thy brother was a furtherer in the act.
Thou art pinched for 't now, Sebastian. Flesh
　　and blood,
You, brother mine, that entertained ambition,　　75
Expelled remorse and nature; whom, with Sebastian,
Whose inward pinches therefor are most strong,
Would here have killed your King – I do forgive thee,
Unnatural though thou art. Their understanding
Begins to swell; and the approaching tide　　　80
Will shortly fill the reasonable shore,
That now lies foul and muddy. Not one of them
That yet looks on me, or would know me. Ariel,
Fetch me the hat and rapier in my cell.
I will discase me, and myself present　　　　85
As I was sometime Milan. Quickly, Spirit!
Thou shalt ere long be free. (ARIEL *sings and helps*
　　him to dress.)

ARIEL

　　　　Where the bee sucks, there suck 1.
　　　　In a cowslip's bell I lie;
　　　　There I couch when owls do cry.　　　90
　　　　On the bat's back I do fly
　　　　After summer merrily.
　　　Merrily, merrily shall I live now
　　　Under the blossom that hangs on the bough.

98 *mariners* sailors.

99 *Under the hatches* below deck.

100 *enforce* bring them by force.

101 *presently* straight away.

    I prithee I beg you.

103 *Or ere* before.

105 *Inhabits* exists.

108 *For more assurance* in order that you should be certain.

111 *thou be'st* you are.

    no not.

113 *late* recently.

    not do not.

115 *Th' affliction of my mind amends* my mental confusion decreases.

116 *crave* need.

PROSPERO

Why, that 's my dainty Ariel! I shall miss thee;   95
But yet thou shalt have freedom. So, so, so.
To the King's ship, invisible as thou art.
There shalt thou find the mariners asleep
Under the hatches. The master and the boatswain
Being awake, enforce them to this place,   100
And presently, I prithee.

ARIEL

I drink the air before me, and return
Or ere your pulse twice beat.

Exit

GONZALO

All torment, trouble, wonder and amazement
Inhabits here. Some heavenly power guide us   105
Out of this fearful country!

PROSPERO

                Behold, sir King,
The wrongéd Duke of Milan, Prospero.
For more assurance that a living prince
Does now speak to thee, I embrace thy body;
   (Embraces ALONSO)
And to thee and thy company I bid   110
A hearty welcome.

ALONSO

             Whether thou be'st he or no,
Or some enchanted trifle to abuse me,
As late I have been, I not know. Thy pulse
Beats, as of flesh and blood; and, since I saw thee,
Th' affliction of my mind amends, with which,   115
I fear, a madness held me. This must crave –

117 **An if this be at all**   if this is not just a dream but is real.

118–9 **Thy dukedom I resign . . . Thou**   I give up my right to serve in your dukedom and beg you to.

119–20 **how should Prospero Be**   how is it that you are.

122 **be**   is truly happening.

123–4 **You do yet . . . subtleties o'**   you are still coming across the magic of.

126 **were I so minded**   if I so wished.

127 **pluck his highness' frown**   cause the king to frown.

132 **rankest fault**   worst, most evil.

133 **perforce**   by force.

An if this be at all – a most strange story.
Thy dukedom I resign, and do entreat
Thou pardon me my wrongs. But how should Prospero
Be living and be here?

PROSPERO

          (To GONZALO) First, noble friend,   120
Let me embrace thine age, whose honour cannot
Be measured or confined. *(Embraces him)*

GONZALO

             Whether this be
Or be not, I 'll not swear.

PROSPERO

            You do yet taste
Some subtleties o' the isle, that will not let you
Believe things certain. Welcome, my friends all!   125
(Aside to SEBASTIAN *and* ANTONIO) But you, my brace
    of lords, were I so minded,
I here could pluck his highness' frown upon you,
And justify you traitors. At this time
I will tell no tales.

SEBASTIAN

        (Aside) The devil speaks in him.

PROSPERO

                  No.
(To ANTONIO) For you, most wicked sir, whom to
    call brother   130
Would even infect my mouth, I do forgive
Thy rankest fault – all of them – and require
My dukedom of thee, which perforce, I know,
Thou must restore.

134 **thou be'st**   you are.

135 **particulars**   the details.

thy preservation   the way you were kept alive.

136 **since**   ago.

137 **wracked**   shipwrecked.

138 **sharp**   painful.

remembrance   memory.

140 **irreparable**   impossible to make better, beyond repair.

140–1 **and Patience . . . cure**   it will not get better in time or with patience.

142 **her**   i.e. Patience.

143 **like**   similar.

145 **late**   recent.

146 **dear**   painful.

147–8 **I Have lost my daughter**   Prospero is presumably referring to the fact that Miranda will be lost to him when she marries Ferdinand.

149 **that**   if only.

151 **oozy bed**   i.e. the sea-bed.

ALONSO

              If thou be'st Prospero,
Give us particulars of thy preservation,   135
How thou hast met us here, who three hours since
Were wracked upon this shore; where I have lost –
How sharp the point of this remembrance is! –
My dear son Ferdinand.

PROSPERO

              I am woe for 't, sir.

ALONSO

Irreparable is the loss; and Patience   140
Says it is past her cure.

PROSPERO

             I rather think
You have not sought her help, of whose soft grace
For the like loss I have her sovereign aid,
And rest myself content.

ALONSO

             You the like loss!

PROSPERO

As great to me, as late; and, supportable   145
To make the dear loss, have I means much weaker
Than you may call to comfort you, for I
Have lost my daughter.

ALONSO

            A daughter?
O heavens, that they were living both in Naples,
The king and queen there! That they were, I wish   150
Myself were mudded in that oozy bed
Where my son lies. When did you lose your daughter?

154 **encounter** meeting.

admire stand amazed.

155 **devour** literally 'eat up', meaning lose all sense of.

scarce think cannot believe.

156 **do offices** give evidence.

157 **natural breath** ordinary speech.

howsoe'er however it is that.

158 **justled** knocked.

159 **that very** the very same.

160 **Which** who.

162 **yet** for the moment.

164 **relation** story.

165 **Befitting** suitable for.

166 **my court** i.e. where he conducts his daily business like a king at court.

attendants who serve me.

169 **requite** repay.

170 **wonder** spectacle.

172 **play me false** aren't playing fairly.

174–5 **a score . . . fair play** Miranda suggests that offered twenty kingdoms Ferdinand would be bound to play false and she would, because of her love for him, call it fair.

PROSPERO

In this last tempest. I perceive these lords
At this encounter do so much admire
That they devour their reason, and scarce think   155
Their eyes do offices of truth, their words
Are natural breath. But, howsoe'er you have
Been justled from your senses, know for certain
That I am Prospero, and that very duke
Which was thrust forth of Milan; who most
        strangely   160
Upon this shore, where you were wracked, was
        landed,
To be the lord on 't. No more yet of this;
For 't is a chronicle of day by day,
Not a relation for a breakfast, nor
Befitting this first meeting. Welcome, sir;   165
This cell 's my court. Here have I few attendants,
And subjects none abroad. Pray you, look in.
My dukedom since you have given me again,
I will requite you with as good a thing;
At least bring forth a wonder, to content ye   170
As much as me my dukedom.

Here PROSPERO *discovers* FERDINAND *and* MIRANDA *playing
chess.*

MIRANDA

Sweet lord, you play me false.

FERDINAND

                            No, my dearest love,
I would not for the world.

MIRANDA

Yes, for a score of kingdoms you should wrangle,
And I would call it fair play.

211

176 **A vision**   some unreal image created by magic.

180 **compass thee about**   surround you.

181 **Arise**   stand up.

    thou cam'st   you came to be.

183–4 **Oh brave . . . people in 't!**   having grown up on the island Miranda has never seen so many people before.

183 **brave**   splendid.

184 **'T is new to thee**   there is perhaps a note of cynicism here, 'when you know more you'll feel differently: humans are not so wonderful'.

185 **thou wast**   you were.

186 **Your eld'st . . . three hours**   you can only have known each other for three hours at the most.

187 **severed us**   torn us apart, in the storm.

188 **mortal**   human, not a goddess.

189 **immortal Providence**   heavenly good fortune.

ALONSO

                         If this prove   175
A vision of the island, one dear son
Shall I twice lose.

SEBASTIAN

                A most high miracle!

FERDINAND

Though the seas threaten, they are merciful;
I have cursed them without cause. *(He kneels)*

ALONSO

                  Now all the blessings
Of a glad father compass thee about!   180
Arise, and say how thou cam'st here.

MIRANDA

                     Oh wonder!
How many goodly creatures are there here!
How beauteous mankind is! Oh brave new world,
That has such people in 't!

PROSPERO

             'T is new to thee.

ALONSO

(To FERDINAND*)* What is this maid with whom
      thou wast at play?   185
Your eld'st acquaintance cannot be three hours.
Is she the goddess that hath severed us,
And brought us thus together?

FERDINAND

               Sir, she is mortal;
But by immortal Providence she 's mine.
I chose her when I could not ask my father   190

193 *renown*   reports, rumours.

195 *Received a second life*   Ferdinand suggests he died when his father perished and Miranda brought him back to life again.

196 *him*   i.e. Prospero.

I am hers   she has my loyalty.

199 *burthen our remembrances*   burden our memories.

200 *A heaviness that's gone*   a past sorrow.

200 *inly*   inwardly.

201 *Or*   otherwise I.

ere   before.

203 *chalked forth*   marked out.

205 *issue*   children, descendants.

For his advice, nor thought I had one. She
Is daughter to this famous Duke of Milan,
Of whom so often I have heard renown,
But never saw before; of whom I have
Received a second life; and second father   195
This lady makes him to me.

ALONSO

                I am hers.
But, oh, how oddly will it sound that I
Must ask my child forgiveness!

PROSPERO

                    There, sir, stop.
Let us not burthen our remembrances with
A heaviness that 's gone.

GONZALO

                I have inly wept,   200
Or should have spoke ere this. Look down, you
   gods,
And on this couple drop a blessed crown!
For it is you that have chalked forth the way
Which brought us hither.

ALONSO

              I say, Amen, Gonzalo!

GONZALO

Was Milan thrust from Milan, that his issue   205
Should become kings of Naples? Oh, rejoice
Beyond a common joy! and set it down
With gold on lasting pillars: in one voyage
Did Claribel her husband find at Tunis,
And Ferdinand, her brother, found a wife   210

213 **was his own**   was in full control of his senses.

214 **still**   forever.

214–5 **his heart That**   the heart of that person who.

217–8 **I prophesied . . . drown**   see note to Act 1, scene 1, line 29.

218–9 **blasphemy . . . o'erboard**   at the start of the play Gonzalo commented on
the boatswain's swearing, which was so marked that grace left the ship.

223 **but three . . . out split**   only three hours ago we thought was wrecked.

224 **tight and yare**   sound, not leaking, and ready.

bravely   finely.

225 **put**   set.

226 **tricksy**   nimble and magical.

Where he himself was lost, Prospero his dukedom
In a poor isle, and all of us ourselves
When no man was his own.

ALONSO

      (To FERDINAND *and* MIRANDA) Give me your hands.
Let grief and sorrow still embrace his heart
That doth not wish you joy!

GONZALO

                Be it so! Amen!   215

Enter ARIEL, *with the* MASTER *and* BOATSWAIN, *astonished,*
following.

Oh, look, sir, look, sir! Here is more of us.
I prophesied, if a gallows were on land,
This fellow could not drown. Now, blasphemy,
That swear'st grace o'erboard, not an oath on shore?
Hast thou no mouth by land? What is the news?   220

BOATSWAIN

The best news is, that we have safely found
Our King, and company; the next, our ship –
Which, but three glasses since, we gave out split –
Is tight and yare and bravely rigged as when
We first put out to sea.

ARIEL

      (Aside to PROSPERO) Sir, all this service   225
Have I done since I went.

PROSPERO

      (Aside to ARIEL) My tricksy Spirit!

ALONSO

These are not natural events; they strengthen
From strange to stranger. Say, how came you hither?

229 **well** wide.

230 **strive** try.

dead of sleep fast asleep.

231 **clapped under hatches** locked in below deck.

234 **mo** more.

235 **at liberty** freed.

236 **in all our trim** totally unharmed.

238 **Cap'ring to eye her** dancing about with joy at seeing her.

On a trice in an instant.

240 **moping** in a dulled state.

't it.

241 **diligence** hardworking spirit.

242 **e'er** ever.

243–4 **more than nature . . . conduct of** something beyond the natural i.e. something magical or spirit-led.

244 **oracle** a medium through which the gods would speak.

245 **rectify** correct or complete.

liege sovereign lord.

246 **infest your mind** wrong or preoccupy yourself.

247 **picked** chosen.

248 **Which shall . . . single** which within a short while will be continuous.

248–9 **I'll resolve . . . of every** I shall give you believable explanations for all of it.

BOATSWAIN

    If I did think, sir, I were well awake,
    I 'd strive to tell you. We were dead of sleep,   230
    And – how we know not – all clapped under
      hatches;
    Where, but even now, with strange and several
      noises
    Of roaring, shrieking, howling, jingling chains,
    And mo diversity of sounds, all horrible,
    We were awaked; straightway, at liberty;   235
    Where we, in all our trim, freshly beheld
    Our royal, good, and gallant ship; our Master
    Cap'ring to eye her. On a trice, so please you,
    Even in a dream, were we divided from them,
    And were brought moping hither.

ARIEL

        (Aside to PROSPERO) Was 't well done?   240

PROSPERO

    (Aside to ARIEL) Bravely, my diligence. Thou shalt
      be free.

ALONSO

    This is as strange a maze as e'er men trod.
    And there is in this business more than nature
    Was ever conduct of. Some oracle
    Must rectify our knowledge.

PROSPERO

           Sir, my liege,   245
    Do not infest your mind with beating on
    The strangeness of this business. At picked leisure
    Which shall be shortly single, I 'll resolve you,
    Which to you shall seem probable, of every

250 **till when** until that time.

253 **fares** are you getting along.

254 **yet** still.

256–7 **Every man . . . for himself** everyone makes a plan for us all (it appears to be the opposite of 'every man for himself' and is perhaps an error due to his drunkenness.)

257 **Coragio** have courage.

259 **If these be . . . my head** if my eyes tell the truth.

261 **Setebos** the god worshipped by Caliban's mother Sycorax.

263 **chastise me** punish me.

266 **plain fish** a reference to Caliban as commonplace.

267–8 **Mark out . . . they be true** look at the clothes and say if they are honest (or if they are servants of the king).

268 **misshapen knave** i.e. Caliban.

These happened accidents; till when, be
    cheerful,   250
And think of each thing well. *(Aside to* ARIEL*)* Come
    hither, Spirit.
Set Caliban and his companions free.
Untie the spell. *(Exit* ARIEL*)* How fares my gracious sir?
There are yet missing of your company
Some few odd lads that you remember not.   255

Enter ARIEL, *driving in* CALIBAN, STEPHANO, *and* TRINCULO, *in
their stolen clothing.*

STEPHANO

    Every man shift for all the rest, and let no man
    take care for himself; for all is but fortune. Coragio,
    bully-monster, coragio!

TRINCULO

    If these be true spies which I wear in my head,
    here 's a goodly sight.   260

CALIBAN

    O Setebos, these be brave spirits indeed!
    How fine my master is! I am afraid
    He will chastise me.

SEBASTIAN

             Ha, ha!
    What things are these, my lord Antonio?
    Will money buy 'em?

ANTONIO

             Very like. One of them   265
    Is a plain fish, and, no doubt, marketable.

PROSPERO

    Mark but the badges of these men, my lords;
    Then say if they be true. This misshapen knave,

271 **without**   forces beyond, i.e. devils.

275 **thing of darkness**   evil creature.

276 **pinched to death**   severely punished.

278 **Where had he wine?**   where did he get the wine?

279 **reeling ripe**   so drunk that he is unsteady on his feet.

280 **gilded**   coated.

281 **pickle**   drunken mess. There follows a play on words when Trinculo picks
   up its other meaning, as a preservation, from line 282.

283–4 **I shall not fear fly-blowing**   as well-pickled meat he is so well preserved that
   the flies will not come near him.

286–7 **but a cramp**   full of pain.

287 **sirrah**   a form of address for inferiors.

His mother was a witch; and one so strong
That could control the moon, make flows and
    ebbs,   270
And deal in her command, without her power.
These three have robbed me; and this demi-devil –
For he 's a bastard one – had plotted with them
To take my life. Two of these fellows you
Must know and own; this thing of darkness I   275
Acknowledge mine.

CALIBAN

                    I shall be pinched to death.

ALONSO

Is not this Stephano, my drunken butler?

SEBASTIAN

He is drunk now. Where had he wine?

ALONSO

And Trinculo is reeling ripe. Where should they
Find this grand liquor that hath gilded 'em?   280
How cam'st thou in this pickle?

TRINCULO

I have been in such a pickle, since I saw you last,
that, I fear me, will never out of my bones. I shall
not fear fly-blowing.

SEBASTIAN

Why, how now, Stephano!   285

STEPHANO

Oh, touch me not! I am not Stephano, but a
cramp.

PROSPERO

You 'd be king o' the isle, sirrah?

289 *a sore one*   a severe king (or perhaps one in pain).

290 *a strange*   as strange as.

291–2 *disproportioned in his . . . shape*   as ugly in his personality as in his body.

294 **To have . . . handsomely**   if you hope to be forgiven then tidy, or decorate, it well.

295 *hereafter*   from now on.

296 **seek for grace**   look for forgiveness.

299 **bestow your luggage**   put back your clothing, trappings.

301 *train*   followers.

303 *waste*   spend.

304 *discourse*   conversation.

STEPHANO

    I should have been a sore one, then.

ALONSO

    (Pointing to CALIBAN*)* This is a strange thing as
        e'er I looked on.   290

PROSPERO

    He is as disproportioned in his manners
    As in his shape. Go, sirrah, to my cell;
    Take with you your companions; as you look
    To have my pardon, trim it handsomely.

CALIBAN

    Ay, that I will; and I 'll be wise hereafter,   295
    And seek for grace. What a thrice-double ass
    Was I, to take this drunkard for a god,
    And worship this dull fool!

PROSPERO

                  Go to; away!

ALONSO

    Hence, and bestow your luggage where you found it.

SEBASTIAN

    Or stole it, rather.   300

          Exeunt CALIBAN, STEPHANO, *and* TRINCULO

PROSPERO

    Sir, I invite your Highness and your train
    To my poor cell, where you shall take your rest
    For this one night; which, part of it, I 'll waste
    With such discourse as, I not doubt, shall make it
    Go quick away: the story of my life,   305
    And the particular accidents gone by
    Since I came to this isle. And in the morn

308 *nuptial*   marriage.

310 *solemnized*   formally carried out and blessed.

311 *retire me*   I will return.

312 *Every third . . . my grave*   I shall think a great deal about death.

314 *Take the ear strangely*   make a strange story.

315 *auspicious*   driven by favourable omens.

316 *expeditious*   speedy.

317 *far off*   which is now far off.

   chick   dear one.

I 'll bring you to your ship, and so to Naples,
Where I have hope to see the nuptial
Of these our dear-belovéd solemnized;   310
And thence retire me to my Milan, where
Every third thought shall be my grave.

ALONSO

           I long
To hear the story of your life, which must
Take the ear strangely.

PROSPERO

        I 'll deliver all;
And promise you calm seas, auspicious gales, 315
And sail so expeditious, that shall catch
Your royal fleet far off. *(To* ARIEL*)* My Ariel, chick,
That is thy charge. Then to the elements
Be free, and fare thou well! *(To* ALONSO*)* Please
 you, draw near.

             Exeunt

1 *o'erthrown*   ended.

4 *confined by you*   kept by the audience.

8 *by your spell*   the audience has the power to keep the actors on stage.

9–10 *But release . . . good hands*   clap, and so end my service to you.

16–18 *Unless I be . . . all faults*   unless you show me mercy and release me.

19–20 *As you from . . . me free*   give me the forgiveness you would want for
yourself. (The phrase is like the words of The Lord's Prayer 'Forgive us
our trespasses as we forgive those who trespass against us'.)

Epilogue

Spoken by PROSPERO.

Now my charms are all o'erthrown,
And what strength I have 's mine own,
Which is most faint. Now 't is true
I must be here confined by you,
Or sent to Naples. Let me not,   5
Since I have my dukedom got
And pardoned the deceiver, dwell
In this bare island by your spell
But release me from my bands
With the help of your good hands.   10
Gentle breath of yours my sails
Must fill, or else my project fails,
Which was to please. Now I want
Spirits to enforce, Art to enchant;
And my ending is despair,   15
Unless I be relieved by prayer,
Which pierces so that it assaults
Mercy itself and frees all faults.
   As you from crimes would pardoned be,
   Let your indulgence set me free.   20

Exit

■ Study programme

Before reading the play

Plot

It has been argued that Shakespeare was influenced in the structure of the plot of **The Tempest** by two traditions in play writing: the neo-classical idea of unity and the Jacobean court masque.

The neo-classical idea of unity

The structure of classical plays was determined by following three basic rules:

- **Place** The stage could only represent one place, thus all the action of the play must occur in one setting. The audience should not be expected to believe that one stage represented more than one country or district.

- **Time** The play should show the passing of a limited amount of time, no more than twenty-four hours. The audience should not be expected to believe that weeks, months or years were passing.

- **Action** The action of the play should be a single plot which determined the way in which each scene of the play developed.

If all these elements existed then the play could be described as following a Neo-Classical unity.

The Jacobean Court Masque

This was a dramatic form developed in Shakespeare's time as an amusement for the king or queen. It was a short scene, often with music, dance and dialogue, which had a single message. The masque used dramatic and impressive costumes and was designed to be performed only once or twice, for a specific purpose. Sometimes they would be performed in the garden of a manor house as the king and queen walked through the grounds, or in court when a foreign visitor wished to be entertained.

▣ As you watch or read through this play, note down the extent to which Shakespeare follows these two traditions. Is the play set in one place, with a single basic plot from which all action develops? How much time passes in the play? Are there any scenes which appear to be like masques; dramatic and spectacular performances given to convey a single message?

The Tempest is sometimes described as a Romance, sometimes as a Pastoral and sometimes as a Tragi-comedy. Here are some brief descriptions of these styles of play.

Romance

A romance in Shakespeare's time was a romantic comedy in which characters might have to go through trials but will eventually find love, and by the end of the play, be set to marry and live happily together.

Pastoral

This was a play set in the countryside, away from the court. The setting was often shown as idyllic, with nature in all its beauty and simplicity. Characters would be introduced into this scene who were out of place. Thus noblemen, kings, queens, princes or princesses, might live as commoners unaware of their noble birth, or individuals established in court life might be forced into living in this unfamiliar territory. The setting enabled the play to explore whether being of noble or lowly birth dictates one's behaviour (*nature*), or whether it is the manner in which one has been raised (*nurtured*).

Tragi-comedy

Guarini, an Italian writer whose work was known in England in Shakespeare's time, believed in writing to a particular format where the opposites of tragedy and comedy were brought together in a play. Before this the two types of play had been seen as separate, whereas Guarini saw each act of the play as having a particular function:

Act 1: A necessary and pressing issue which needs to be resolved is presented. There must be tragic and comic action to prepare the audience for the mix of the two throughout the play.

Act 2: New information must be introduced, which is linked, but perhaps not directly, to the plot.

Act 3: The focus should be comic, giving an intricate plot.

Act 4: The action of the plot should come to a climax, where tragedy appears almost certain to happen.

Act 5: The happy ending must be brought out of potential tragedy.

2 One of the key aspects of Shakespeare's work is that although he often used themes, plots and characters previously used by others, he never did so without making some changes to them. Read through the summaries given at the start of each act of the play, and, working with a partner or group, identify the extent to which **The Tempest** fits these three forms.

As you watch or read through the play take note of the extent to which the play is a Romance, a Pastoral or a Tragi-Comedy, noting also the ways in which it varies from all three. You could feed your ideas back to the group in a talk or display.

Character

1 The characters in **The Tempest** can be grouped in various ways. Using the character list on page 3 try to list the characters within the following groups:
- humans and non-humans
- people of noble birth and people of ordinary birth
- servants and masters
- previous residents of Italy and island inhabitants
- male and female

As you watch or read through the play you can see to what extent your assumptions were correct. You can also make up some other categories by which to group the characters such as evil characters/good characters, young/old etc.

2 Many exam questions on **The Tempest** will ask you to write about a single character in the play and/or the inter-relationship of two or three characters. Work with a partner or small group to draw up a standard list of things it would be useful to know about a character in the play, in order to comment on them and their relationships. Here are some ideas to get you started:

- name;
- social position;
- role in the plot;
- what happens to him/her in the plot;
- what others say about him/her.

When you have established a basic list use this as a guideline for keeping notes on characters in the play. Remember to be specific in your note-taking, recording exact act, scene and line references for useful quotations.

Themes

1 **The Tempest** is a play which touches on many themes some of which are recorded below. Work with a partner or group to brainstorm what these themes mean to you and the different ways they may be developed in a story.

- Nature versus nurture: are people bound to develop in a particular way because of their birth and breeding or does it depend more on how they are treated and what they are taught?
- Colonisation: what right do people have to set up a society where others have established a way of living? Do they have the right to 'civilise' the land or should they leave it as it is?

- Reality versus Illusion: how can you tell what is real and what is an illusion created by acting or magic?
- Leadership: what makes a good or bad leader?
- Revenge or forgiveness: how should people who have behaved badly be treated? Is revenge justifiable or should we always forgive?
- Chaos and order: how does the chaotic become ordered and the ordered become chaotic?
- Death of a relative
- Love – at first sight
    - between parents and children
    - between brothers
    - between servants and masters
- The loss of a dukedom
- What makes a good or bad servant?
- Magic
- Freedom versus duty.

As you progress through the play take note of the ways in which these themes develop.

During reading

Act I

Check your knowledge of Act I

- What is happening on board the king's ship at the start of the play? Who is the most powerful person on the ship in these circumstances and why?
- What does Miranda ask Prospero to do at the start of scene 2, and how does Miranda feel about the storm and the sailors?
- What does Miranda remember about life before she arrived on the island?

- How did Prospero lose his dukedom in Milan?
- How did Miranda and Prospero survive being cast out of Milan? Who in particular helped them?
- What has Ariel been doing and who has commanded him?
- What are Caliban's complaints against Prospero? What are Prospero's complaints against Caliban?
- Who does Ferdinand think Miranda is when he first sees her and what news has he just received himself?

Questioning the text in Act 1

1. The play begins with a storm and apparent shipwreck where the king and his son believe each other to be dead, and all those who were on board are thrown into confusion. Pick out those events in the Act which suggest that chaos will continue and those which suggest that some harmony will be reached.

   Work with a partner to predict how the chaos might develop or how the harmony might be restored. As you continue through the play notice the extent to which your predictions come true.

2. In this Act Prospero tells the story of his past life in Milan. Work with a partner or group to produce a time-line of events in Prospero and Miranda's lives which have occurred before the play begins.

   On the same line mark in the events which have occurred in the lives of the other characters, as and when you find out about them in the play. Continue the time-line to indicate what happens in the course of the play. You will need to design the line in such a way that it indicates how little time is covered in the play and how much passes in the events which occur before it begins.

3. Miranda and Caliban have both grown up on the island. Miranda is the daughter of a nobleman, Caliban the son of a witch, Sycorax, and a devil. In terms of breeding it is suggested that Miranda could not be more noble nor Caliban more lowly born. Both are given

nurturing from Prospero. Look closely at Act 1, scene 2, lines 127–174 and lines 281–376 and complete a chart of the similarities and differences between Miranda and Caliban's treatment and their response to it.

Miranda		Caliban	
Prospero's treatment	*Miranda's response*	*Prospero's treatment*	*Caliban's response*
was taught by Prospero as a schoolmaster teaches a pupil	learned well, and became better educated than a princess	given water with berries in it.	showed Prospero the island
		allowed to sleep in Prospero's cell	tried to rape Miranda

As you progress through the play make a note of the ways in which Shakespeare suggests nurturing can influence nature and the ways it cannot.

4 What impression do you have of Prospero so far in the play? Work with a partner or in two groups, one of which defends Prospero and his actions the other of which accuses Prospero of behaving unfairly. Each person or group should collect evidence from the text to support the viewpoint they hold.

As you progress through the play continue to collect evidence for and against Prospero (and perhaps other characters such as Caliban or Alonso).

At various points during your work you could set up a debate to consider each view leading to a final vote or trial at the end of the play.

Act 2

Check your knowledge of Act 2

- How do Sebastian and Antonio respond to Gonzalo's attempts to comfort Alonso?
- Why is Alonso grieving?
- What do Sebastian and Antonio plan while the other courtiers are asleep?
- Why is Caliban serving Prospero even though it is against his wishes?
- What does Caliban think Stephano is, and vice versa?
- What does Trinculo see when he enters in scene 2?
- What has Trinculo got that Caliban wants and what does he offer in order to have his share of it?

Questioning the text in Act 2

1 What impression do you have of the island so far? Write the word 'island' in the centre of a piece of paper and brainstorm what you have learnt about it. The diagram at the top of page 238 gives you some idea of where to start.

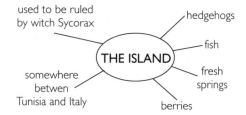

When you have completed the brainstorm identify the character who has given each piece of information about the island:

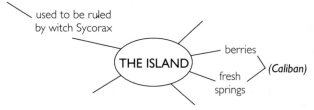

As you progress through the play you can add more information, and perhaps complete sketches or collect magazine photographs which you think might resemble the island as it is described. Keep in your mind the question 'Who has the greatest right to live and rule on the island?'

2️⃣ What have you learnt about the relationship between masters and servants by the end of Act 2? Think about the relationships between:

- the boatswain and Gonzalo
- Prospero and Ariel
- Ariel and Sycorax
- Sebastian/Antonio and Alonso
- Gonzalo and Alonso
- Caliban and Stephano/Trinculo

What is your impression so far of:

- the nobility
- the servant classes?

Discuss with a partner which relationship is best and worst, giving your reasons. What makes a good servant and a good master?

3️⃣ Humour plays an important part in this Act, as we are shown by the clever word-play in scene 1 of the noblemen Antonio and Sebastian, who mock Gonzalo, and, in scene 2, the visual humour of Stephano's discovery of Caliban and the subsequent arrival of Trinculo.

Look again at one or other of these episodes and try acting it out in a small group in order to produce the greatest comic effect. When you have completed your scene hold a meeting to decide what has made the scene funny, identifying the elements which were necessary to create the humour. Here are some ideas to start you off:

Antonio and Sebastian scene

- Antonio and Sebastian speak in low voices so that Gonzalo cannot hear them.
- a running joke – like the bet in lines 27–40.

Trinculo and Stephano scene

- confusion – who's who?
- fear in the characters when there is nothing to fear.

As you progress through the play take note of other comic scenes, identifying what causes the humour.

Act 3

Check your knowledge of Act 3

- What task is Ferdinand performing for Prospero and why?

- How does Prospero react when he realises that Ferdinand and Miranda have fallen in love?

- How does Caliban describe Prospero to Stephano and Trinculo?

- What does Ariel do whilst invisible in the company of Stephano, Trinculo and Caliban and what is the effect of his actions?

- Stephano and Trinculo are scared of the music of the island. How does Caliban reassure them?

- What is given to and taken from the nobles in the third scene?

- In what shape does Ariel appear to the noblemen, and what are they told by Ariel?

Questioning the text in Act 3

▨ Magic has an important part to play in **The Tempest**. Drawing on your knowledge of the first three Acts of the play decide which of the following phrases are true and which are false:

- Prospero has the magic power to use Ariel but not to control him;

- Prospero can control the weather on and near the island;

- Sycorax used magic over Ariel;

- Prospero has magic so powerful that it can make people think and feel in certain ways;

- Prospero has learned his magic from books;

- Prospero can control the island spirits;

- Prospero does not use his magic on Miranda;

- Caliban does not understand Prospero's magic;

- Prospero can make Ariel produce magical music;

- Prospero does not use his magic to hurt people.

Work with a partner to make up some more true and false statements about magic in the play.

▨ What impression have you got of love so far in the play? Discuss with a partner what you have noticed about the love between:

- Fathers and daughters
- Fathers and sons
- Brothers
- Friends
- Servants and masters
- Miranda and Ferdinand

You could keep a tape of your conversation or make some spider graphs to show the elements which are unique to each type of love and those which the different types of love might have in common.

3 The characters in **The Tempest** are often confused as to what is real and what is an illusion caused by magic. Chart back through the play and up to the end of Act 3, identifying every event which one or more characters thought was real when it was in fact an illusion, and any event which one or more character thought was an illusion when in fact it was real.

Keep filling in more information on to the chart as you move through the play.

THOUGHT REAL ACTUALLY ILLUSION	THOUGHT ILLUSION ACTUALLY REAL
Act 1, scene 1: Sailors and nobleman think it is a real shipwreck. In fact it is an illusion created by Prospero through Ariel (as shown in Act 1, scene 2, lines 190–215).	*Act 1, scene 2:* Ferdinand believes Miranda is a goddess when in fact she is human.

Act 4

Check your knowledge of Act 4

- What reasons does Prospero give Ferdinand for having punished him?

- What spectacle is shown to Ferdinand and Miranda?

- Why does Prospero stop the spectacle, and how does he describe it to Ferdinand?

- What distraction is presented to Stephano and Trinculo which makes them temporarily forget their plotting?

- What is Caliban's reaction to the spectacle?

- What chases Trinculo, Stephano and Caliban off at the end of the scene?

Questioning the text in Act 4

▨ *De Occulta Philosophia* written in 1533 by Cornelius Agrippa was a well known source of information on magic in Shakespeare's time. According to this book, supernatural power was divided into three levels:

- The ability to control the natural world and its elements, and the basic actions of people.

- The ability to control the stars and planets.

- The ability to control spirits and intelligences.

Caliban's mother, Sycorax, represents what the Elizabethans saw as black magic – in witchcraft linked to the devil and used for evil purposes. Prospero represents the Elizabethan view of white magic, as practised by the magus – a magician who has learnt magic from books of magic and who uses it to serve good purposes.

Trace back through the play, looking at Act 4 in particular, to identify how many of these levels can be controlled by Sycorax and how many by Prospero. Make a note of Act, scene and line references which prove your theories.

Take note also of any references which suggest that Sycorax practises black magic and Prospero white magic.

Do you think there are any occasions when Prospero abuses his magical art?

2 In the first scene of this Act, Prospero reveals why he has made Ferdinand act as his slave, putting him on trial in order to earn Miranda's love. Look closely at lines 1–31. Then look at Act 1, scene 2, lines 377–496 and at Act 3, scene 1, lines 1–91. Do you think Prospero is justified in acting as he does? What does this situation tell us about Ferdinand?

What other characters in the play have been put on trial by Prospero? How have they met the test?

3 Much of Act 4 is taken up with the spectacular masque which Prospero creates to celebrate Miranda and Ferdinand's union. Look closely at the words spoken by Ceres, Iris and Juno in order to explore the following ideas:

- What does the masque tell you about:
    - the goddesses, the duties they perform and the aspects of nature to which they are related?
    - the love between Ferdinand and Miranda?
    - the future which is promised for Miranda and Ferdinand?
- Why do you think Prospero causes this particular masque to appear?

4 Look closely at Prospero's words in Act 4, scene 1, lines 145–65. What new information does this give you about:

- the character of Prospero
- magic
- life, as Prospero sees it?

Act 5

Check your knowledge of Act 5

- Who persuades Prospero to act with compassion towards the noblemen?
- What does Prospero plan to give up and what will he do to symbolise this?
- What task does Prospero give Ariel to perform while he addresses the noblemen?
- What does Prospero tell Alonso he has recently suffered? How is this true?
- How does Miranda respond to seeing the noblemen?
- What news does the boatswain bring to the company?
- What does Caliban promise at the end of the Act?

Questioning the text in Act 5

1 *The Tempest* is a play about power. As you read the end of the play consider the following:
  - Who has lost power in or before the play?
  - Who has increased their power in or before the play?
  - Who uses their power for good?
  - Who uses their power for evil?
  - Who has the most power at the start of the play?
  - Who has the most power by the end of the play?
  - What gives power to those who are most powerful?

  If you had to elect a ruler from those characters present, who would you choose and why?

2 Prospero takes it upon himself to set up a situation in which he will have the opportunity to meet with, challenge, judge and punish those who have wronged him in the past. It has been suggested by critics that Prospero's actions are full of the highest principles. To

what extent does Prospero treat his enemies with justice, mercy and forgiveness? To what extent is his behaviour effective in getting his enemies to repent and seek forgiveness? Do you think it is right to manipulate people in this way? You could chart your thoughts as indicated below:

Enemy	Treatment	Response
ALONSO	Makes him believe his son is dead; confronts him via Ariel as harpy.	Mourns; recognises his wrong-doing towards Prospero and seeks forgiveness. Lavishes love on Prospero's child.

3 Look again at your notes about servant and master relationships (see Questioning the text in Act 2, assignment 2). Reflecting on the play as a whole what new things have you learnt about relationships by the end of the play? Choose any one relationship and in a short essay, explore:

- how it changed through the course of the play;
- how it stands at the end of Act 5;
- the effect the relationship has on each of the two individuals.

Epilogue

1 Some have argued that through Prospero, Shakespeare is making his farewell to the stage, as **The Tempest** was probably the last play he wrote alone, and the last he worked on in performance in

London, before returning to Stratford. These critics maintain that Shakespeare's art of the imagination was being shown and explored through Prospero's art as a magician.

Looking at the Epilogue on page 229 and the play as a whole, pick out any scenes where you think Shakespeare might be bidding farewell to imagination, writing, the stage, or perhaps even life itself.

After reading

Plot

▨ Read through the Act summaries again with a partner. They are only sketches of the action, so as you read, take it in turns to explain what happens more fully, making some brief notes as you talk. In each scene ask yourselves the following questions:

- How many plots are there?
- How does the play move from one plot to another?
- What type of scene is this – comic, sad, concerned with love, a magic spectacle, a scene which retells a story, a chaotic scene, a harmonious scene?

Use this information to make your own flow chart of the action of the play. The example shown on page 247 gives you one idea of how your chart might begin, but you may find a better way to show how the action moves. Could you show the action as all one plot? If so what might the plot be called?

STUDY PROGRAMME

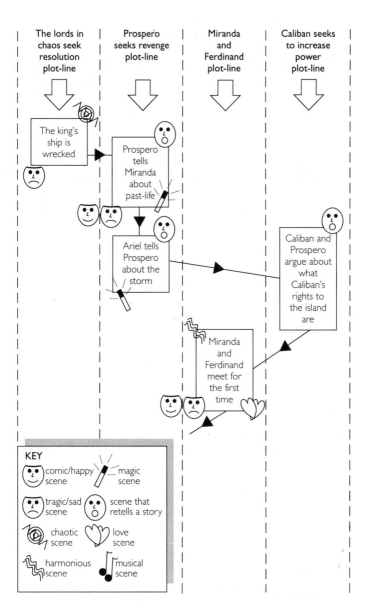

247

2 Refer back to the Before reading section on Plot (pages 230–32) and the work you did in Assignments 1 and 2. Now that you have read the play say to what extent you think this play is a Neo-Classical plot, a Jacobean masque, a Romance, a Pastoral, a Tragi-Comedy or a combination of all these elements. Give references to support your view.

3 Look at some plot summaries from some other plays by Shakespeare in the Longman Literature series. You might like to consider *A Midsummer Night's Dream* and *Twelfth Night*, to begin with. Having read the summaries draw a diagram which shows the similarities and differences between the plays. It might begin rather like the one below:

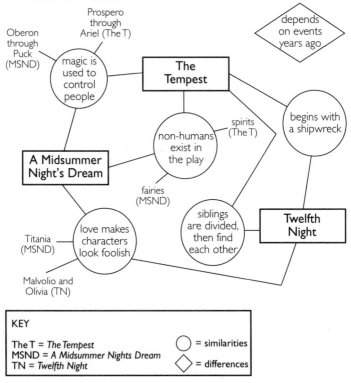

KEY

The T = *The Tempest* ◯ = similarities
MSND = *A Midsummer Nights Dream* ◇ = differences
TN = *Twelfth Night*

Character

▨ The following quotations are descriptions of Caliban and Ariel which have been made by critics writing about **The Tempest**.

He has all the discontents, and malice of a witch, and of a devil, besides a convenient proportion of the deadly sins; gluttony, sloth, and lust, are manifest; the dejectedness of a slave is likewise given him, and the ignorance of one bred up in a desert island. His person is monstrous, and he is the product of unnatural lust; and his language is as hobgoblin as his person; in all things he is distinguished from other mortals.

John Dryden, 1679

The very first words uttered by this being introduce the spirit, not as an angel, above man; not a gnome, or a fiend, below man; . . . In air he lives, from air he derives his being, in air he acts; and all his colours and properties seem to have been obtained from the rainbow and the skies.

S. T. Coleridge, 1811

He is neither born of heaven, nor of earth; but, as it were, between both, like a May-blossom kept suspended in air by the fanning breeze, which prevents it from falling to the ground.

S. T. Coleridge, 1811

He is a sort of creature of the earth . . . He partakes of the qualities of the brute, but is distinguished from brutes in two ways: – by having mere understanding without moral reason; and by not possessing the instincts which pertain to absolute animals. Still X is in some respects a noble being: the poet has raised him far above contempt: he is a man in the sense of the imagination: all the images he uses are drawn from nature, and they are highly poetical . . . No mean figure is employed, no mean passion displayed, beyond animal passion, and repugnance to command.

S. T. Coleridge, 1811

Identify which quotations refer to Caliban and which to Ariel.

Using the character information you have collected whilst reading the play, work in a group to prepare an illustrated talk in which you explore the differences between the characters of Ariel and Caliban. Consider each in terms of:

- their appearance
- their powers
- their relationship with Prospero, Miranda, Sycorax, Stephano and Trinculo
- their role in the play
- their attitude to servitude and freedom.

Illustrate your talk talk by:

- giving sketches of the characters
- quoting their words
- acting out short excerpts from the play.

2 Which characters behaves badly during the play? Working alone or in a small group, prepare a speech for the defence and for the prosecution of one character in the play who you think could be accused of behaving badly.

Set up a trial in which individuals in the class role-play different characters who can be questioned about the behaviour of the character who is accused. Decide as a class who is the most reprehensible character in the play in words, thoughts or actions. Then write up a report of the trial in which you argue whether you feel the decision made was correct, backing up your ideas with reference to the text.

3 Learn by heart any single speech in the play. Present your speech and prepare yourself to answer questions on any of the following:

- the meaning of words or phrases spoken
- the general context of this speech in the scene, Act and play as a whole.
- the character who is speaking, what the speech reveals about him or her, and your impressions of him or her in the play as a whole.

4 Imagine you are one of the characters writing your memoirs ten years after the events of the play have taken place. Making close reference to the text reflect on what happened to you on the island, what your feelings were at the time, and what you now understand that you would only have guessed at then.

5 Prospero has brought the noblemen to the island in order to put right the wrong he believes he was done by them. Write a detailed character study of Prospero, with close reference to the text, and using short, apt quotations where appropriate. The writing might include:

- his role in the plot
- his use of magic
- his relationship with others: consider in particular his relationship with Miranda, Caliban, Gonzalo and Ariel
- his treatment of others: consider in particular his treatment of Ferdinand, Caliban, Alonso and Antonio
- his motives for acting as he does – was he justified?
- his state of mind at the beginning and end of the play.

To what extent do you find him an interesting, sympathetic and believable character?

Themes

1 On page 252 is a diagram of some of the themes in **The Tempest**. Using your notes made whilst reading the play, write your own theme chart which gives as much textual information as possible. You might like to do this as a whole group, covering a display wall with your ideas. Having finished the chart use it to:

- give a presentation about the themes in the play (if you work as a whole class you could give a group presentation to another class, illustrated with acted excerpts or illustrations.)
- choose one theme and write a detailed account of the ways in which this theme is explored in the play.

- make an argument for one theme being more important than any other in the play and then hold a debate to consider which theme is the most important. You will have to have detailed references to the text to support your ideas.

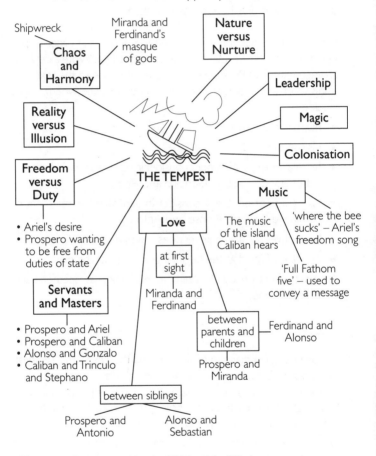

2 Walter Raleigh, writing in 1907, said of Shakespeare:

The indispensible preliminary for judging and enjoying Shakespeare is not knowledge of his history, not even knowledge of his works, but knowledge of his theme, a wide acquaintance with human life and human passion as they are reflected in a sensitive and independent mind.

To what extent do you think the themes of **The Tempest** can be summed up in this way?

3 Shakespeare shows us different experiences of loss and grieving in **The Tempest**. What are the similarities and differences between the mourning we see in:

- Ferdinand for his father
- Alonso for his son
- Prospero for his dukedom
- Caliban for 'his' island?

Write up your views in a short critical essay, complete with relevant quotations.

4 Read some sonnets by Shakespeare written on a similar theme to one which is present in **The Tempest**. Write a comparison of the sonnets you find. Common themes you might like to consider are love, death and old age.

Language

The Tempest has some of Shakespeare's most memorable speeches. They are rich in compressed imagery (see the section on images in Shakespeare's language on page xix). Much of the language is musical just as the island itself.

Read out the following lines (Act 1, scene 2, lines 399–407):

Full fathom five thy father lies;
   Of his bones are coral made;
Those are pearls that were his eyes.
   Nothing of him that doth fade,
But doth suffer a sea-change
Into something rich and strange.

Sea-nymphs hourly ring his knell.
  Ding-dong.
Hark! Now I hear them – ding-dong, bell.

Below you will see that the passage is repeated again but that this time notes have been added, showing some of the stylistic features in the writing. The box which follows the passage will help you with the technical terms used.

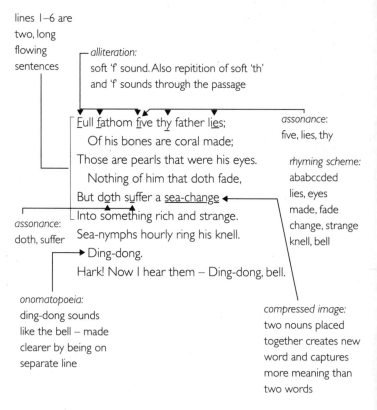

lines 1–6 are two, long flowing sentences

alliteration:
soft 'f' sound. Also repitition of soft 'th' and 'f' sounds through the passage

Full fathom five thy father lies;
  Of his bones are coral made;
Those are pearls that were his eyes.
  Nothing of him that doth fade,
But doth suffer a sea-change
  Into something rich and strange.
Sea-nymphs hourly ring his knell.
  Ding-dong.
  Hark! Now I hear them – Ding-dong, bell.

assonance:
five, lies, thy

rhyming scheme:
ababccded
lies, eyes
made, fade
change, strange
knell, bell

assonance:
doth, suffer

onomatopoeia:
ding-dong sounds like the bell – made clearer by being on separate line

compressed image:
two nouns placed together creates new word and captures more meaning than two words

Alliteration: the repetition of the same initial sounds in words placed closely together.

Assonance: the rhyming of vowel sounds in words placed closely together.

Rhyming scheme: to show how a verse rhymes, name the first line *a* then any other lines which rhyme with this line are also *a*. When you have a new rhyming sound name it *b* and so on through the alphabet. In this extract the rhyme becomes ababccded.

Compressed image: where an idea is expressed in a few words. In this case 'sea-change' means the change that the movement of the sea brings about to make stone and shell into sand or, in a magical way, turns bones into coral.

Onomatopoeia: a word which sounds like the sound it is seeking to describe. In the case of this extract 'ding-ding' sounds like a bell when spoken out loud.

Repetition: where a word or words are repeated to create an effect. In this extract a sense of echo is created by repeating the words 'ding-dong'.

▨ Following the example given above, make a copy of the following extracts from the play, and add notes to show your understanding of the stylistic features:
- Act 1, scene 2, lines 1–13
- Act 3, scene 2, lines 137–45
- Act 4, scene 1, lines 106–117
- Act 4, scene 1, lines 146–163.

Shakespeare also uses language to create pictures in the audience's mind. Look at the following extract from a speech made by Prospero in Act 4, scene 1, lines 148–58. He is explaining how the spectacle Ferdinand and Miranda have been watching is a masque rather than a real appearance of goddesses, and that in the same way life itself is merely a performance. Notes have been added to identify some of the images used, and the techniques which have created the image.

> Our revels now are ended. These our actors,
> As I foretold you, were all spirits, and
> Are melted into air, into thin air.
> And, like the baseless fabric of this vision,
> The cloud-capped towers, the gorgeous palaces,
> The solemn temples, the great globe itself,
> Yea, all which it inherit, shall dissolve,
> And, <u>like this insubstantial pageant faded</u>,
> <u>Leave not a rack behind. We are such stuff</u>
> <u>As dreams are made on</u>; and <u>our little life</u>
> <u>Is rounded with a sleep.</u>

simile:
life is like
an insubstantial
pageant (a masque or
play performance) – it fades
and leaves nothing behind

metaphor:
the end of
our life (death) is
compared to the end
of each day (sleep)

Simile: comparing one object to another object. The comparison often uses the phrases 'as . . . as' or 'like a'.

Metaphor: making a comparison of two objects by saying one is the other.

Personification: giving human qualities to an inanimate object.

---

2 As well as identifying assonance and alliteration, see how many types of imagery you can find in the following passages from the play:
- Act 1, scene 2, lines 217–24
- Act 2, scene 1, lines 270–4
- Act 3, scene 3, lines 53–60
- Act 4, scene 1, lines 146–63.

3. In addition to the plays, Shakespeare wrote a set of celebrated sonnets. They can be found in any **Collected Works of Shakespeare**.

A *sonnet:* a poem of fourteen lines with ten beats in each line. Shakespeare's sonnets have a rhyming scheme of *abab, cdcd, efef, gg*. The meaning of the poem is often divided into two parts, like two stages to an argument. Sometimes this divides the poem up into eight lines and six lines and sometimes into twelve lines and two lines.

The following sonnets consider themes which are also in **The Tempest** and they all use similar stylistic techniques and imagery. Look up the sonnets and then compare them with the extracts from the play identified alongside. What themes and stylistic features are similar?

Sonnet (XIII) 13:   Act 1, scene 2, lines 424–30
                               Act 3, scene 1, lines 1–15

Sonnet (CXVI) 116: Act 3, scene 1, lines 66–91

Sonnet (XCIV) 94:   Act 5, scene 1, lines 8–32

4. Write your own sonnet which might have been written by one character in **The Tempest** to another.

Performance

We can immensely increase our delight in Shakespeare, and strengthen our understanding of him if . . . we keep asking ourselves how the thing was done.

Quiller-Couch

The first recorded performance of **The Tempest** was on All Saints Day (the days following Halloween), 1 November 1611, in the Banqueting House at Whitehall. This was a performance in front of the King, James 1, who always attended the first command performance of the winter season given by The King's Men, the company with whom Shakespeare worked.

The Banqueting House was generally used for the performance of masques – short spectacular scenes, which used scenery and machinery to move it around and thus produce transformations.

There is no existing account of this performance, but we do know something of how the room looked, from a review of a play performed in the same space in January 1618:

> A large hall is fitted up like a theatre, with well secured boxes all round. The stage is at one end and his Majesty's chair in front under an ample canopy. Near him are stools for the foreign ambassadors . . . Whilst waiting for the King we amused ourselves by admiring the decorations and beauty of the house with its two orders of columns . . . The whole is of wood, including even the shafts, which are carved and gilt with much skill. From the roof of these hang festoons and angels in relief with two rows of lights . . . although they profess only to admit the favoured ones who are invited, yet every box was filled notably with most noble and richly arrayed ladies, in number some 600 and more according to the general estimate . . . On [the King] entering the house, the coronets and trumpets to the number of fifteen or twenty began to play very well a sort of recitative.
>
> In John Russell Brown's, *Shakespeare: The Tempest: Studies in English Literature*

The Tempest is a short play (only **The Comedy of Errors** is shorter), and it was known that James I did not like long performances. It is also suggested that Prospero may have been created to, in some way compliment the King, himself a scholar of magic. Also at the performance may well have been Queen Anne and Prince Henry (James' heir) who were used to dancing in the masques and who enjoyed music, which may explain why there is so much music in the play.

Thus the play may have been written with the acting space and the court audience in mind, or perhaps adapted for this performance having been previously written for use in The Globe (a public playhouse seating 2000) and Blackfriars (a private playhouse with fewer seats and a more exclusive audience) both of which were being used for performances by The King's Men at this time (see 'Where were Shakespeare's plays performed?' page xi).

There was another court performance of **The Tempest** in 1613, as part of the marriage celebrations of the king's daughter Elizabeth to Prince Frederick of Bohemia.

When the actors and company put together the first folio of Shakespeare's works in 1623 (after Shakespeare's death), **The Tempest** was placed first in the collection. This may well have been because it was a popular play with audiences of the time. It was known by a wide public and in tune with a popular form of romantic tragi-comedy being produced by the younger contemporary writers Beaumont and Fletcher. It also contained similar elements to the popular masques written by Ben Johnson at the time.

Unlike other plays in the folio, **The Tempest** is heavily edited with more punctuation, stage direction, costume suggestions and ideas for stage business than any other play. This may be because Shakespeare himself was perhaps less involved in the productions of **The Tempest** and thus others were having to keep note of how the play was to be directed and staged.

There are also two events which suggest that Shakespeare was taking a different role with regard to his plays, reverting to a more personal life and preparing for retirement. Firstly, in May 1609 his sonnets were published for the first time in book form. These were deeply personal accounts of love as experienced by Shakespeare some years before. They revealed more to the public about Shakespeare the man than his plays had done previously.

Secondly it is believed that in 1610 Shakespeare left London and returned to live in Stratford, in order to prepare for retirement from the theatre. There he lived in New Place with his wife and daughter (until she married in 1616) and near his other married daughter Suzanna Hall. He lived in a pastoral setting, owning 107 acres of land himself at the time.

Using the information above complete any of the following tasks:

▦ Sketch out plans for and then build, a model of the inside of the Banqueting House at Whitehall as you believe it would have looked on All Saints Day 1611. Keep a written log of how you go through the process of creating the finished design.

2 Design a portfolio of the costumes you think would have been worn by the players for this performance. Give reasons for your choices, and justify them in the light of the information above, some research into Elizabethan dress and your knowledge of the play. Make the designs as exciting as you can, perhaps using swatches of material to give a clearer idea of your intention. You could produce one of the costumes to be worn!

3 Draw some designs for the tapestries which might have been hung around the hall to give a flavour of the play. Carry out some research into Elizabethan embroidery and art, and perhaps attempt to make a life-sized collage or painting.

4 Look closely at the text of **The Tempest** in order to speculate on how the machinery of the theatre might have been used to create various spectacular effects. Make sketches of scenes and machinery that might have been used.

5 Design a programme for the performance which might have been given to King James 1, Queen Anne and Prince Henry to give them a flavour of the play they were about to see.

6 What implications does the information about **The Tempest** in performance have for the shape and content of the play? Prepare a talk in which you consider the influence these facts would have had on Shakespeare's writing of the play if he had designed it for this particular performance.

7 Carry out some research into the Globe Theatre, and Blackfriars Theatre. You should try to discover:

- who would be likely to attend a performance in each;
- what differences existed in terms of the structure of the buildings, and how these might affect performances;

- what differences existed in terms of the laws regulating perform-ances, because of their different locations;
- what differences existed in terms of the acting company and additional players available in each playhouse.

You could then make a display of sketches, notes and 3D models showing how these things would have affected performances of *The Tempest*.

Further assignments

These assignments are particularly suitable for advanced level students.

Yet Shakespeare was a man, and a writer: there was no escape for him; when he wrote, it was himself that he related to paper, his own mind that he revealed.
Walter Raleigh, 1907

The Tempest is thought to have been the last play that Shakespeare wrote on his own. He probably wrote it in 1610 or 1611 and it was probably first performed in 1611, when he was 48 years old. He died in 1616. What do you think the play reveals about Shakespeare the playwright, and Shakespeare the man? For comparison look at **King John**, the play which was believed to be the first he wrote. What evidence is there in the characters, themes and plot, that **King John** was written by a young man and **The Tempest** by a man near the end of his life?

The following quotations also made about Shakespeare may help:

Shakespeare is above all writers, at least above all modern writers, the poet of nature; the poet that holds up to his readers a faithful mirror of manners and of life.

Ben Johnson

I find it impossible to deny that Prospero is, to some extent, an imaginative paradigm of Shakespeare himself in his function as poet; and that he does in part embody Shakespeare's self-awareness at the conclusion of his poetic career.
J. Middleton Murry, 1936

Lytton Strachey in his famous essay 'Shakespeare's final period' (1906) reacted strongly against such idealizing of the late plays by debunking them both as works of art and as products of mature contentment, insisting that Shakespeare at the end of his career was 'bored with people, bored with real life, bored with drama, bored, in fact, with everything except poetry and poetical dreams'.

Sandra Clark, ***Shakespeare: The Tempest,***
Penguin Critical Studies, 1986

2 ***The Tempest*** is often grouped with three other plays by Shakespeare: ***Pericles***, ***Cymbeline*** and ***The Winter's Tale***, which collectively are known as The Late Plays, as they were believed to be written at the end of Shakespeare's life.

In his essay 'The Serenity of The Tempest', written in 1875, Edward Dowden says:

Over the beauty of youth and the love of youth, there is shed, in these plays of Shakespere's final period, a clear yet tender luminousness, not elsewhere to be perceived in his writings. In his earlier plays, Shakespeare writes concerning young men and maidens, their loves, their mirth, their griefs, as one who is among them, who has a lively, personal interest in their concerns, who can make merry with them, treat them familiarly, and, if need be, can mock them into good sense. There is nothing in these early plays wonderful, strangely beautiful, pathetic about youth and its joys and sorrows . . . in these latest plays, the beautiful pathetic light is always present. There are the sufferers, aged, experienced, tried . . . . And over against these there are the children absorbed in their happy and exquisite egoism.

Spend some time looking at plot summaries, extracts, performances or the complete text of one or all of the other late plays by Shakespeare. What themes, ideas, character types, morals do these plays have in common? To what extent is ***The Tempest*** similar to and different from these other plays?

(If you are working as a whole class you could divide into groups to research different plays, and then find some lively and interesting ways to present your findings to the rest of the group. These could form the basis of a written project on the plays.)

▣ One of the themes of **The Tempest** is that of colonisation. There are various sources which Shakespeare would almost certainly have drawn on to form the plot of this play.

- William Strachey wrote a pamphlet in 1610 (which Shakespeare almost certainly saw before its publication in 1625), called 'A True Reporatory of the Wrack'. It told of a sea voyage made by Sir Thomas Gates (with William Strachey on board), which, in May 1609, set out to colonise Virginia, with a fleet of nine ships and six hundred passengers. Sir Thomas Gates' ship was caught in a hurricane and wrecked near the island of Bermuda. This was an area greatly feared by travellers, who believed the islands were inhabited by devils.

  It was a terrible storm and the ship did get badly damaged, but miraculously, the crew and passengers managed to survive. The Bermudas were not at all the islands that the travellers had expected to find, being full of wildlife, fresh water and all they needed to survive. Sir George Somers, the admiral of the fleet, set everyone to work on building a ship so that they could sail on to Virginia in the following spring.

  A small group began a mutiny, as they wanted to stay on the islands, some planned to kill the governor, but the leader of the mutiny was executed and the rest kept under strict rule by Somers. They eventually sailed on to Virginia, arriving in May 1610, much to the surprise of the colonists who had already begun living there. They had not survived so well; three hundred had died over the winter from famine and disease poorly controlled, Strachey suggests, due to a lack of leadership.

  Another account of this voyage 'A True Declaration' by Bullough, states:

  Every man overvaluing his own worth, would be commander: everyman underprizing an others value, denied to be commanded.

- Florio wrote a translation of Montaigne's essay 'Of the Canniballes' which was published in 1603. Montaigne was interested in the colonising of North America, and wrote the essay based on information from his servant who had lived there. He saw the behaviour of natives, even cannibals as only barbaric if viewed from the eyes of over-civilised Elizabethans. Viewed differently, he argued, the North Americans could be seen as living the pure, simple and honest pastoral life of 'The Golden Age' which poets revered. Speaking of the North American Indians he stated:

> . . . what in those nations we see by experience, dost not only exceed all the pictures wherewith licentious Poesie hath proudly imbellished the golden age, and all her quaint inventions to faine a happy condition of men, but also the conception and desire of Philosophy. They could not imagine a genuitie so pure and simple, as we see it by experience: nor ever beleeve our society might be maintained with so little art and humane combination.

In what ways do you think these publications might have influenced Shakespeare in the characters, plot and themes of **The Tempest**?

In order to research your ideas you might like to look at:

- Caliban's descriptions of the island;
- the character of Caliban;
- Gonzalo's ideal commonwealth;
- Prospero's leadership.

Present your findings as a talk or illustrated report on the sources of the play.

4 Perhaps because **The Tempest** relies so much upon action which takes place before the play begins, we often respond by wondering what might happen after the end of the play.

Some interesting sequels can be found in **The Virgin Queen** by F. G. Waldron and **The Sea and the Mirror** by W. H. Auden. You might like to research these before completing the task of writing your own sequel for **The Tempest**. Your story script should:

- relate in some way to the action which has already taken place in the play;
- involve some or all of the characters from **The Tempest**, and they

must continue to act in character, following on from how they have been in Shakespeare's play;

- give some insight into the tensions which exist at the end of the play such as:
  - the journey home;
  - what will happen on the island after the nobles have gone;
  - whether Antonio will abide by Prospero's rules once Prospero has given up his magic.

Study questions

Many of the activities you have already completed will help you to answer the following questions. Before you begin, it may be useful to consider these important guidelines about essay writing:

- Spend some time deciding exactly what the essay question is asking. It may be useful to break the sentence down into phrases or words and decide what each part means.

- Focusing on the areas you have decided are relevant, note down as many quotations or references to the play as you can think of, which are relevant to the answer.

- Decide on a shape which you think will be appropriate for the essay. It may be useful to think of a literal shape which will suit the argument.

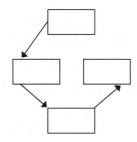 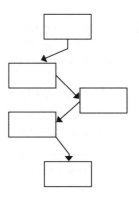

- Organise your ideas and quotations into sections to fit your shape, you could do this literally by placing notes into different piles.
- Write a draft of your essay.
- Redraft as many times as you need to, taking care to consider the following:

  Does this answer the questions?

  Is this essay easy to read, with clear organisation in which one point flows on to another?

  Do the opening and concluding paragraphs seem clear and linked to the question set?

  Are there any spelling/grammatical errors? Use a dictionary and the thesaurus.

1. What impression are we given of the island from the different characters' experiences of it in *The Tempest*?

2. To what extent does *The Tempest* move from a state of chaos to a state of harmony?

3. Discuss the different forms and uses of magic in *The Tempest*.

4. When he first sees Prospero in Act 5, scene 1 Gonzalo says 'Whether this be or be not, I'll not swear.' To what extent is this state of mind understandable at this point of the play?

5. Shakespeare's language is rich in meaning and sound. Choose any two or three extracts from *The Tempest* to illustrate the richness of Shakespeare's language.

6. J. Middleton Murry states in his essay 'Shakespeare's Dream':

   In The Tempest Shakespeare wants to make clear what he means: that men and women do not become their true selves by Nature merely, but by Nurture.

   Discuss this statement in relation to your understanding of nature and nurture in the play.

7 *Prospero is a ruler and **The Tempest** is a study in power: spiritual and temporal; natural and supernatural; power over the outer world and power over the self.*
Sandra Clark, **Penguin Critical Studies: The Tempest,** 1986

Discuss this statement with close reference to the text.

8 Miranda is the only woman we see in **The Tempest**. What do we learn from her about Elizabethan women, their position in society, their desires, strengths and weaknesses?

9 Who, in your opinion, has the greatest right to rule a) on the island and b) in Milan. Defend your beliefs with reference to the text, exploring as you do so, the elements necessary to make a good ruler.

10 Discuss the different types of love, service and friendship shown in **The Tempest**. Who, in your opinion, shows the greatest love?

11 Which character or characters did you find the most interesting in the text? Present a study of any one or two characters, using close reference to the text to explore the ways in which they interested you.

12 Discuss the various ways in which music is used and presented in **The Tempest**. To what extent do you think music is necessary in the play?

Using part of the text

Below are two suggestions for using just a part of the text of **The Tempest**. You do not need to have read or seen the whole play in order to complete them.

▓ This Island's Mine

In Act I, scene 2, lines 310–376, the audience meets the character of Caliban. He has been described earlier as the child of a devil and a witch, who was banished to an enchanted island. Miranda and Prospero have lived on the island with Caliban for twelve years, having been shipwrecked there. Ariel is a spirit of the air used by Prospero to perform magic. Ariel wants his freedom and complains to Prospero. Caliban too feels he should be free and indeed that he should rule the island.

- Read through the scene in a group of five, with four of you reading character parts and the fifth reading stage instructions.

- Talk as a group about your impressions of each character and the relationship between the different characters. Make sure everyone understands the gist of what is being said.

- Position yourselves to act out part of the scene without words. The person who has read out stage instructions can act as director, watching the action and suggesting alternative gestures and movements as appropriate.

- On a second run-through you should have an idea of what is being said in the scene so add in some ad-libbed words and/or some of the actual words, but you should not, as far as possible look at the text.

- Return to a planning meeting and decide what costumes you want each character to wear, what props, if any, are needed, and how you might create the impression of the island with simple staging or lighting.

- Divide the tasks between the group and agree on a deadline by which time they will be completed.

- Perform the scene to an audience. You could do this as an ad-libbed script, or agree to learn the words by heart.

- Make a suitable programme for the audience.

- Ask the audience to participate in some way. Perhaps they could judge whether Prospero's treatment of Ariel is fair.

You could also choose a scene from another of Shakespeare's plays which shows the relationship of servants and masters. Here are some you might consider:

- Act 3, scene 2 of *A Midsummer Night's Dream* and the relationship of Oberon and Puck.
- Act 3, scene 1 of *Othello* and the relationship of Othello and Iago.
- Act 1, scene 3 of *Romeo and Juliet* and the relationship of the Nurse and Lady Capulet.

2 A Musical Island

Look at Act 3, scene 2, lines 137–45. *The Tempest* is set on an enchanted island that is full of music. Caliban, an inhabitant of the island understands its music and is able to reassure Trinculo and Stephano, two drunken servants of the king who have been shipwrecked on the island, that there is nothing to fear.

- Work with a group to look closely at the passage spoken by Caliban.
- Collect together or design and make some musical instruments that you could use to create the strange island music.
- Make a tape recording of the words of the passage with the music accompanying it.
- You could carry out the same exercise on other musical extracts from the play such as:
  - Act 1, scene 2, lines 377–89
  - Act 1, scene 2, lines 399–407
  - Act 2, scene 2, lines 183–8
  - Act 3, scene 3, lines 18–20 (and stage directions)
  - Act 4, scene 1, lines 106–17
  - Act 4, scene 1, lines 134–8 (and stage directions)
  - Act 5, scene 1, lines 88–94.

Pearson Education Limited
Edinburgh Gate, Harlow,
Essex CM20 2JE,
and Associated Companies throughout the world

First published 1994
Fourteenth impression 2007

Editorial material set in 10/12 point Gill Sans Light
Printed in Malaysia, GPS

The Publisher's policy is to use paper manufactured from
sustainable forests.

ISBN 978-0-582-22583-1

Acknowledgements
Cover illustration by Reg Cartwright

Photographs on pages 4, 66, 124, 164 and 194 © Donald Cooper,
Photostage.